B.C. Science PROBE 4

Authors

Anita Chapman
Educational Consultant and Author,
Chapman & Associates Educational Consulting Inc.

Carmen Dawkins
North Okanagan-Shuswap School District (#83), B.C.

Burt Deeter
Surrey School District (#36), B.C.

Brian Herrin
Intermediate Teacher,
Formerly of West Vancouver School District (#45), B.C.

Carol Roitberg
North Vancouver School District (#44), B.C.

Program Consultant

Arnold Toutant
Educational Consultant,
A. Toutant Consulting Group Ltd.

THOMSON

NELSON

Australia   Canada   Mexico   Singapore   Spain   United Kingdom   United States

THOMSON

NELSON

B.C. Science Probe 4

Authors
Anita Chapman
Carmen Dawkins
Burt Deeter
Brian Herrin
Carol Roitberg

Program Consultant
Arnold Toutant

Director of Publishing:
Beverley Buxton

Acquisitions Editor, Science:
John Yip-Chuck

Executive Managing Editor, Development:
Cheryl Turner

Project Manager, Science:
Lois Beauchamp

Program Manager:
Lee Geller

Project Editor:
Lee Ensor

Developmental Editor:
Janis Barr

Editorial Assistants:
Alisa Yampolsky, Jacquie Busby

Executive Managing Editor, Production:
Nicola Balfour

Senior Production Editor:
Deborah Lonergan

Copy Editor:
Gilda Mekler

Proofreader:
Susan McNish

Indexer:
Noeline Bridge

Senior Production Coordinator:
Sharon Latta Paterson

Creative Director:
Angela Cluer

Art Director:
Ken Phipps

Text Design:
Kyle Gell Design

Art Management:
Kyle Gell, Allan Moon

Composition Team:
Kyle Gell, Allan Moon

Cover Design:
Peter Papayanakis

Cover Image:
A.G.E Foto Stock/First Light

Illustrators:
Steven Corrigan
Deborah Crowle
Kyle Gell
Kathy Karakasidis
Dave Mazierski
Allan Moon
Jenna Moon
Kayleigh Paterson
Bart Vallecoccia
Dave Whamond

Photo Researcher:
Mary Rose MacLachlan

Printer:
Transcontinental Printing Inc.

**Library and Archives Canada
Cataloguing in Publication**

B.C. science probe 4 / authors, Anita
Chapman ... [et al.].

Includes index.
ISBN 0-17-628272-6

1. Science—Texbooks. I. Chapman,
Anita II. Title: B.C. science probe four.

Q161.2.B38 2006   500   C2005-
905808-4

Reviewers

Aboriginal Education Consultant

Mary-Anne Smirle
Peachland Elementary School,
Central Okanagan School District (#23),
B.C.

Accuracy Reviewers

Gordon Gore
Formerly of Kamloops/
Thompson School District (#73), B.C.
Operator, BIG Little Science Centre,
Kamloops

Marianne Larsen
Formerly of Sunshine Coast School
District (#46), B.C.,
Greater Vancouver Regional Science Fair

Pat Wong
Senior Meteorologist,
Meteorological Service of Canada,
Environment Canada
Pacific and Yukon Region

Assessment Consultant

Anita Chapman
Educational Consultant and Author,
Chapman & Associates Educational
Consulting Inc.

ESL Consultant

Vicki McCarthy, Ph.D.
Dr. George M. Weir Elementary School,
Vancouver School District (#39), B.C.

Literacy Consultant

Sharon Jeroski
Educational Consultant and Author,
Horizon Research and Evaluation, Inc.

Literacy Reviewer

Kyme Wegrich
Glen Elementary School,
Coquitlam School District (#43), B.C.

Numeracy Consultant

Bob Belcher
Happy Valley at Metchosin Elementary
School,
Sooke School District (#62), B.C.

Professional Development Consultant

Brian Herrin
Intermediate Teacher, Formerly of West
Vancouver School District (#45), B.C.

Safety Consultant

Laura Roche
Bayside Middle School,
Saanich School District (#63), B.C.
Executive, British Columbia Science
Teachers' Association

Technology Consultant

Al Mouner
Millstream Elementary School,
Sooke School District (#62), B.C.

Combined Grades Consultant

Susan Martin
Cliff Drive Elementary School,
Delta School District (#37), B.C.

**Advisory Panel and Teacher
Reviewers**

Doug Adler
Department of Curriculum Studies,
Science Education, University of British
Columbia

Kevin Amboe
Surrey School District (#36), B.C.

David Barnum
Sunshine Coast School District (#46),
B.C.

Wade Blake
Rutherford Elementary School,
Nanaimo-Ladysmith School District (#68),
B.C.

Jean Bowman
Saanich School District (#63), B.C.

Lorraine Hoodicoff
Helen Gorman Elementary School,
Central Okanagan School District (#23),
B.C.

Pat Horstead
Mount Crescent Elementary School,
Maple Ridge-Pitt Meadows School
District (#42), B.C.

Jillian Lewis
Lyndhurst Elementary School,
Burnaby School District (#41), B.C.

Selina Millar
Boundary Park Elementary School,
Surrey School District (#36), B.C.

Karen Morley
North Surrey Learning Centre,
Surrey School District (#36), B.C.

Noreen Morris
Trafalgar Elementary School,
Vancouver School District (#39), B.C.

Janice Novakowski
Richmond School District (#38), B.C.

William Shaw
Educational Consultant/Teacher and
Author, B.C.

Heather Stannard
Khowhemun Elementary School,
Cowichan Valley School District (#79),
B.C.

Patricia Tracey
Formerly of Abbotsford School
District (#34), B.C.
Fraser Valley Regional Science Fair
Foundation

Darlene Vissers
Abbotsford School District (#34), B.C.

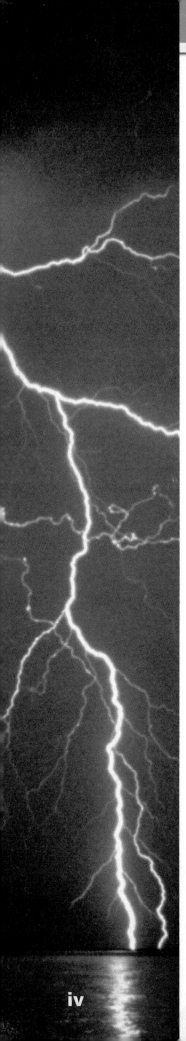

Contents

Chapter 3

UNIT B: LIGHT AND SOUND

UNIT C: HABITATS AND COMMUNITIES

Expanding the World of Science

What is science?

Shaylene,
Shuswap Nation:
Science is fun
because you learn
about lots of
animals. Some don't
have names yet!

Cameron:
It's cool because
you learn a lot and
some day you might
be able to go out
into space.

Tylor,
Westbank
First Nation:
Nuclear science
makes you smarter
when you study.

Jayde,
Blood Band, Alberta:
Science, to me, is like
in bridge building—it
doesn't have to look
pretty, it just needs
to be strong!

Dalton,
Métis Nation:
Science, to me, is
an exploration of
everything in the
world.

Science is what we have learned about our world through exploration and observation. Sometimes scientists do experiments to learn more about what they are studying. Sometimes those experiments are done in laboratories. Sometimes those experiments are done in nature.

Different groups of Aboriginal peoples have lived in parts of British Columbia for generations. Aboriginal peoples have learned many things about the animals, the plants, the weather, and the land close to their homes. This information is a very important part of science.

This information, known as **Indigenous Knowledge** (IK) or Traditional Ecological Knowledge (TEK), was passed to the next generation through stories and songs. Now this information is being written down because it can help all people learn better ways to live in our world.

In British Columbia, as in other places around the world, more and more scientists are asking to work with and learn from Aboriginal peoples and their communities. It is important to Aboriginal peoples that their ways are respected and valued by others. We can all learn from the information that Aboriginal peoples have to share.

Mary-Anne Smirle
Métis Nation
L'Hirondelle clan

Weather

Preview

Every day you make decisions because of the weather! When you were getting ready for school this morning, did you put on shorts or long pants? When you go home, will you want an ice-cold drink or a cup of hot chocolate?

The weather is all around us. It affects how we dress, what we eat or drink, what types of activities we plan to do, and what types of plants and animals live near us. Because weather is so important to people, scientists study it to learn more about it and try to predict the future weather.

A scientist who studies the weather is called a meteorologist [MEE-tee-uh-RAWL-uh-jist]. In this unit, you will work like meteorologists and do many of the same things they do. You will learn to observe weather, measure weather, find patterns in weather, and predict the weather. You will also learn how weather affects both living and non-living things.

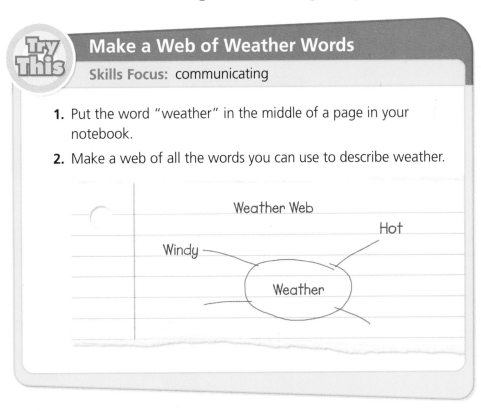

Try This

Make a Web of Weather Words

Skills Focus: communicating

1. Put the word "weather" in the middle of a page in your notebook.
2. Make a web of all the words you can use to describe weather.

Weather Web
Hot
Windy
Weather

◀ A lightning storm over Nanaimo, British Columbia

Chapter 1

We can observe and measure the weather.

➡ Key Ideas

- ▸ The air in our atmosphere can move and can hold water.

- ▸ We can use our senses to observe weather.

- ▸ We can use instruments to measure weather.

- ▸ We can get weather information from many places.

You look out the window in the morning to see if it is sunny or cloudy. You hear rain on the window. You feel the wind on your face as you walk to school. These are observations about the weather.

Sometimes you want more detailed information about the weather. If someone tells you it is warm outside, you might want to know exactly how warm. To get weather information like this, you need to measure using instruments. You can combine your observations and measurements to get a detailed picture of your local weather.

What Is Weather?

Earth is surrounded by a thin blanket of air called the atmosphere [AT-muhs-FEAR]. The day-to-day changes in our atmosphere are called **weather.**

To understand weather, we have to understand the properties of the air in our atmosphere. Air has two important properties:

- It can move.
- It can hold water.

You can see air move. Hold up a piece of paper and blow on it. The paper moves because you are making the air around it move.

In the following activity, you will learn that air can also hold water.

▲ Air can move.

⇨ Learning Tip

Important vocabulary words are highlighted. Make sure you understand what these words mean. Use these words to begin a weather dictionary.

Try This

Find the Water in Air

Skills Focus: observing, inferring

1. Partly fill two glasses with water that is room temperature.
2. Put some ice cubes in one of the glasses.
3. Observe both glasses for 15 minutes.
4. What do you see? Is the same thing happening to both glasses? Where is the water on the outside of the one glass coming from?

▲ This milk bottle was taken out of the refrigerator and left on the counter. Why is it wet?

Water in the Air

Water in the air is called water vapour [VAY-puhr]. You can't see water vapour. When the ice in your glass cooled the air around it, the air became too cool to hold all of the water vapour. So some of the water vapour turned into liquid water on the outside of the glass. This did not happen to the other glass of water because it was the same temperature as the air. The process of water vapour turning into liquid water is called **condensation** [KON-den-SAY-shun].

Where does the water in a puddle go? Some of the liquid water may sink into the ground, but some turns into water vapour in the air. You can see this for yourself. Put some water in a saucer and let it sit on the counter for a few days. The water will disappear. It has changed to water vapour. The process of liquid water turning into water vapour is called **evaporation** [ih-VAP-uh-RAY-shun].

▲ Look at the two photos. The photo on the right shows how much water can evaporate from a saucer of water over a few days.

The Water Cycle

Water is recycled over and over again. We call this the **water cycle.** Warm air rises in the atmosphere. As it rises, it cools. This cooling causes some of the water vapour to condense onto tiny dust particles floating in the air to make water droplets. These water droplets form clouds. The water droplets bump into each other and form larger drops. When the drops get too big, they fall as rain, snow, or hail.

Rain, snow, and hail are all called **precipitation** [prih-SIP-ih-TAY-shun].

Some precipitation evaporates in the heat of the Sun. Some of it collects in the soil, or runs into lakes and rivers. Eventually, all this water flows into the ocean or evaporates back into the air.

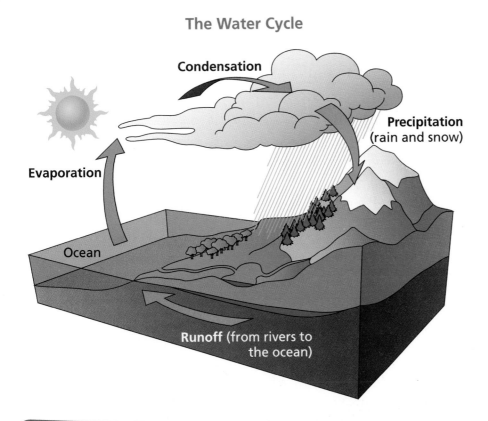

The Water Cycle

Condensation

Evaporation

Precipitation (rain and snow)

Ocean

Runoff (from rivers to the ocean)

⇨ **Learning Tip**

Work with a partner to study this diagram. Start anywhere and follow the arrows. Explain to your partner what is happening to the water at each stage. Then have your partner explain the water cycle to you.

⇨ Check Your Understanding

1. What are two important properties of air?

2. When you cooled the water in your glass, water droplets formed on the outside of the glass. When warm air cools, water vapour condenses to form droplets of water in clouds. Use this information to explain why you can see your breath on a cold day.

3. Draw and label a diagram to show how water from the ocean could travel to a puddle in your schoolyard, then back to the ocean.

Observing and Measuring the Weather

Have you ever stuck out your tongue to let snow fall on it? Do you like the fresh smell in the air after a rain? Have you watched a flag flap in the wind? If so, you have been using your senses to observe the weather.

Observe the Weather

Skills Focus: observing, classifying

1. Make a table like the one below.

I can see the weather.	I can hear the weather.	I can smell the weather.	I can taste the weather.	I can touch the weather.

2. Go outside and observe the weather. Use your eyes. What weather do you see? Write your observations in your table. Now use your other four senses and complete the table.

3. Were you able to make observations using all your senses? Which senses did you use the most? Which senses did you use the least?

4. Compare tables with other students. Which of their observations are the same as yours? Which are different?

Why We Measure Weather

How hot is it today? Your friend might say that it is a warm day. You might think that it's not very warm because you needed a jacket. We all see and feel things differently.

8

Check Your Senses

Skills Focus: observing

1. Put cold water in one container, water that is at room temperature in another container, and warm water in a third container.

 Be sure that the warm water is not too hot!

2. Put one hand in the cold water and the other hand in the warm water. Leave them in the water for a minute.

3. Now put both hands in the room temperature water at the same time. How does each hand feel? How can you explain this?

cold Water

room temperature water

warm water

In this activity, you tricked your brain into thinking that the room temperature water was cool and warm at the same time! When preparing weather reports it would not be useful if one meteorologist thought the weather was cool and another thought it was warm. It is important for all meteorologists to describe the weather in the same way. That is why meteorologists have invented instruments to help them measure the weather accurately.

Check Your Understanding

1. Name all the senses that we can use to observe the weather.

2. Why do meteorologists use instruments to measure weather?

3. If you could use only two senses to observe the weather, which two would give you the most information?

3 Measuring Temperature

Energy from the Sun heats the surface of Earth. The measure of that energy is called **temperature.** The instrument used to measure temperature is called a **thermometer** [thur-MOM-ih-tuhr].

Standard Thermometers

There are many different kinds of thermometers. To measure temperature, you can use a bulb thermometer. When the liquid in the thermometer gets warmer, it takes up more space and rises up the tube. When the liquid gets cooler, it shrinks and the liquid goes down.

The numbers on a thermometer are called the scale. To find the temperature, you read the number on the scale that is at the same height as the liquid.

▲ This is a standard bulb thermometer. What is the air temperature?

▲ To read a thermometer, hold it at eye level to be sure your reading is accurate.

Try This

Practise Using a Thermometer

Skills Focus: measuring

 Be very careful with the thermometers as they are made of thin glass and can break easily. If one breaks, don't touch it. Tell your teacher right away.

1. Use a thermometer to measure the temperature of the air in three places inside your school and three outside. Make a table to record your temperatures.

	3 Places inside my school	Temperature recorded
1.		
2.		
3.		
	3 Places outside my school	
1.		
2.		
3.		

➡ Learning Tip

For a review on measuring temperature, see the Skills Handbook, page 229.

2. Measure carefully. Do not touch the bulb of the thermometer or your hand will warm it up. When you measure the temperature outside, measure in the shade. Stand in each place for at least three minutes to get an accurate reading.

3. Compare your readings with your classmates' readings. Did you get the same readings in the same places?

Minimum-Maximum Thermometers

The air outside is usually warmer in the daytime than at night. Weather reports on television, radio, or in the newspaper report the daily high and low temperatures. You can get these measurements using a minimum-maximum thermometer. These thermometers work by recording the highest and lowest temperatures reached since the thermometer was reset. They can be reset each day by pushing a button. These thermometers also show the current temperature.

↪ **Learning Tip**

Use this labelled diagram to help you read a real minimum-maximum thermometer.

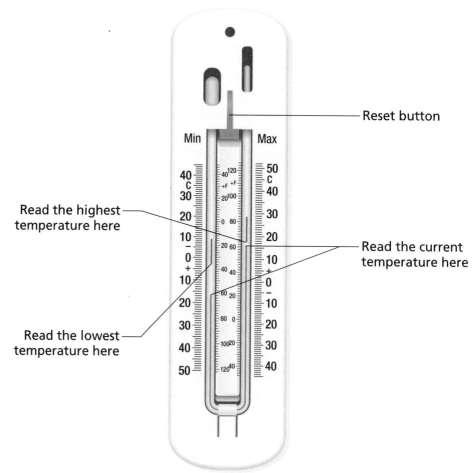

▲ This is a minimum-maximum thermometer. What was the lowest temperature for that day? What was the highest temperature? What is the current temperature?

Anders Celsius invented a scale in 1742. On this Celsius scale, the freezing temperature of water is 0 °C and the boiling temperature of water is 100 °C. This is the same scale that Canada and most of the world uses to measure temperature.

Look at this thermometer. If there were precipitation at this temperature, would it fall as rain or snow?

Check Your Understanding

1. Draw and label three standard bulb thermometers with these temperatures:
   - 30 °C
   - 5 °C
   - −10 °C

   Beside each thermometer, draw pictures to show whether it would be raining or snowing at that temperature and what you might be wearing.

2. Start a table of weather elements and how each is measured. You will add to the table as you work through this chapter.

Weather element	What we use to measure it
temperature	thermometer

Learning Tip

Making a table like this can help you record information as you read.

4 Measuring Precipitation

Measuring Rainfall

You can measure precipitation with simple instruments. The instrument used to measure rain is called a **rain gauge** [RAYN GAYJ]. Rain gauges are containers that catch the rain as it falls. They have a scale that measures the amount of rain in millimetres (mm). You check a rain gauge each day. If there has been rain, you measure it. Then you empty the rain gauge.

▲ These are two common types of rain gauges.

Try This

Measure with a Rain Gauge

Skills Focus: measuring

1. Work with a partner. Take turns putting some water in a rain gauge and reading it in mm. Make sure you read the rain gauge at eye level.

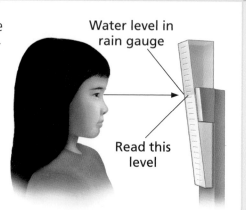

Water level in rain gauge

Read this level

Measuring Snowfall

You can also measure daily snowfall. Choose a flat area away from trees and buildings where the snow will not be disturbed by people shovelling it or walking through it. Use a ruler or a metre stick to measure the depth of the first snowfall in centimetres (cm). Then put a snow board on top of the snow. A snow board is a piece of plywood, about 40 cm by 40 cm. It is used to separate the old snow from the new snow. When it snows again, you can measure the depth of the new snow on top of the snow board.

Sometimes snowfall is difficult to measure because the snow is light and is blown around by the wind. Other times the snow is heavy and wet, and easier to measure.

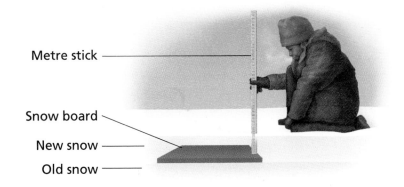

Metre stick

Snow board

New snow

Old snow

◄ This is how you measure how much new snow has fallen.

⇨ Check Your Understanding

1. What might happen if you did not check a rain gauge for several days?

2. Why is it harder to measure snowfall than rainfall?

3. Add to your table.

Weather element	What we use to measure it
temperature	thermometer
rain	
snow	

⇨ Learning Tip

If you do not remember what you can use to measure weather elements, scan the section for illustrations.

5 Measuring Cloud Cover

Make a Cloud

Skills Focus: creating models, observing

1. Get your teacher to pour 1 cm of hot water into a large glass jar. The jar should have a wide mouth and a metal lid.

 Hot water must be handled carefully. Always have an adult pour it for you.

2. Put the metal lid upside down on the jar, and place a few ice cubes on top of the lid.

3. Describe what you see.

In this activity, the ice cubes cooled the air in the jar. This made some of the water vapour in the air condense into water droplets. This is similar to how clouds are formed. A **cloud** is a mass of tiny water droplets that have condensed from water vapour in the air.

Estimating Cloud Cover

Are there clouds in the sky today where you live? How much of the sky do you think is covered by clouds today? People have invented expensive instruments to measure cloud cover from the ground, but human observation is still better. Meteorologists look at the sky and estimate how much of it is covered by clouds. Then they describe the cloud cover in words. Here is a simple Cloud Cover Chart.

Cloud Cover Chart

	Clear	No clouds in the sky.
	A few clouds	Clouds cover one-half or less of the sky.
	Cloudy	Clouds cover more than one-half of the sky.
	Overcast	Clouds cover the whole sky; no blue sky is visible.

Even people who have been observing cloud cover for a long time have difficulty estimating cloud cover. It takes practice, and it helps to work in a group so you can compare your estimates with others.

Estimate Cloud Cover

Skills Focus: creating models, observing, classifying

1. Work with a partner. Get a piece of blue paper from your teacher. This will be your sky.

2. Get smaller pieces of white paper from your teacher. Each piece will be one-quarter of the size of your blue paper. You can choose how many pieces of white paper to take—from one to four. Do not tell anyone else how many you took. You will use these pieces of white paper to make clouds.

3. On the back of your blue paper, write down how many pieces of white paper you took. If you took one, write down $\frac{1}{4}$. If you took two, write down $\frac{2}{4}$ or $\frac{1}{2}$. If you took three, write $\frac{3}{4}$. If you took four, write $\frac{4}{4}$.

4. Tear your pieces of white paper into different shapes of clouds, and glue them to the blue paper. Try not to overlap your clouds.

5. Your teacher will make three signs for these categories of cloud cover: a few clouds, cloudy, and overcast. The signs will be put in different areas of the room.

6. With your partner, hold up your blue paper and ask your classmates to guess how much cloud cover is on it. When someone gets the right answer, go to that area of the room. If you are not sure which area to go to, check the Cloud Cover Chart.

7. When all the models of cloud cover have been classified, go outside and try to estimate the cloud cover in the real sky. Work in groups of four, and try to agree on your estimates. Compare your estimates with those of other groups. Was there much difference in your estimates of cloud cover?

Did you know?

Fog is a cloud that forms near the ground. Fog makes it possible for you to reach out and touch a cloud, or walk in a cloud.

➭ Check Your Understanding

1. A weather report says that it is clear outside. How much of the sky could be covered by clouds?

2. Why is it a good idea to observe cloud cover as a group?

3. How would you describe the cloud cover in each of the following photographs?

➭ Learning Tip

Use the Cloud Cover Chart to help you answer this question or to check your answer.

4. Add to your table.

Weather element	What we use to measure it
temperature	thermometer
rain	
snow	
cloud cover	

6 Measuring Wind

Meteorologists call moving air **wind.** They can measure the wind in three ways. They can measure the effects of wind, the speed of wind, and the direction of wind.

Measuring the Effects of Wind

We can't see the wind, but we can feel it. We can see the effects of wind. Meteorologists sometimes measure the effects of wind using a scale that describes the effects of wind on land and at sea. This scale is called the Beaufort Scale.

The Beaufort Scale

Force	On Land	At Sea
0	Calm, smoke rises straight up	Calm, sea like a mirror
1	Smoke drifts, but weather vanes are still	Ripples only
2	Wind is felt on the face, leaves rustle, weather vanes begin to move	Small wavelets (0.2 m)
3	Leaves and small twigs on trees are constantly moving, flags flap	Large wavelets (0.6 m) crest and fall, but no whitecaps
4	Dust, leaves, and paper on the ground are raised up, small branches in trees move	Small waves (1 m), some whitecaps
5	Small trees with leaves sway	Moderate waves (1.8 m), many whitecaps
6	Large branches of trees move, flags beat	Strong breeze, large waves (3 m), some spray
7	Whole trees sway, resistance is felt when walking against the wind, flags extend straight out	Near gale, larger waves (4 m), foam is blown in streaks downwind
8	Difficult to walk against the wind, twigs and small branches are blown off trees	Gale, moderately high waves (5.5 m), crests break into spindrift (sea spray)
9	Slight damage to buildings, signs blow down, shingles blow off roofs	Strong gale, high waves (7 m), dense foam
10	Trees broken off or uprooted, damage to buildings	Storm, very high waves (9 m), surface of sea generally white
11	Widespread damage to buildings	Violent storm, exceptionally high waves (11 m)
12	Severe destruction	Hurricane, huge waves (14 m)

Measuring Wind Speed

The measure of how fast wind is moving is called
wind speed. The instrument used to measure wind speed
is called an **anemometer** [AN-uh-MOM-ih-tuhr]. The most
common type of anemometer has cups that spin when the
wind blows. The faster the anemometer spins, the higher
the wind speed. A dial on the anemometer shows how fast
the wind is blowing. In Canada, wind speed is measured in
kilometres per hour (km/h).

◀ An anemometer is used to measure wind speed.

Learning Tip

Make a mental picture
of an anemometer in
a strong wind. What
would it be doing?

Try This

Measure Wind Speed

Skills Focus: observing, measuring, interpreting data

1. Go outside and measure the wind speed in two ways—with
   an anemometer and with the Beaufort Scale. What does the
   anemometer tell you about the wind? What does the Beaufort
   Scale tell you about the wind?

2. Compare your measurements with your classmates. Did you
   get the same measurements?

Measuring Wind Direction

We call where wind is coming from **wind direction.** So a south wind comes from the south, a west wind comes from the west, an east wind comes from the east, and a north wind comes from the north.

The instrument used to measure wind direction is called a **weather vane.** Weather vanes are also called wind vanes. Weather vanes have an arrow on them, and as the weather vane turns, the arrow always points into the wind. If the arrow points to the north, then it is a north wind blowing. Sometimes the arrow will point in between two directions, like north and west. That is a northwest wind. If the arrow is in between south and east, that is a southeast wind.

▶ Weather vanes come in many different styles but they all work the same way. Weather vanes are usually put in high places, like on top of buildings. Can you explain why?

Make Your Own Weather Vane

Skills Focus: observing, measuring

1. Work with a partner. Use scissors to cut a slit in each end of a drinking straw.

    Be careful using sharp things like scissors and pins.

2. Attach a small plastic or cardboard triangle to one end of the straw and a larger triangle to the other end.

3. Put a pin through the centre of the straw and into the eraser on the end of a long pencil.

4. Mark the directions on the bottom of a paper cup using the letters N, S, E, and W.

5. Turn the cup upside down and stick the sharp end of the pencil through the cup.

6. Take your homemade weather vane outside. Your teacher will tell you which direction is north, south, east, and west.

7. Hold your weather vane at the end of your arm or tape it to the top of a post. Make sure the directions on the base of your weather vane are facing the right way. What direction is the wind coming from? Remember that the arrow will face into the wind.

Weather Vane

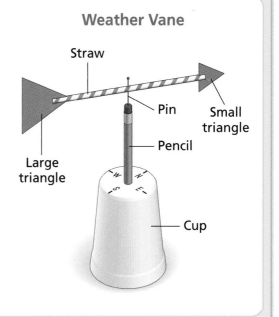

⇨ Check Your Understanding

1. Describe two ways wind speed can be measured. Which way do you prefer? Why?

2. Look at the Beaufort Scale on page 20. If there is a gale warning on the radio, what size waves are expected?

3. Look at the drawing to the right. What would a meteorologist call this wind to tell its direction?

4. Add to your table.

Weather element	What we use to measure it
temperature	thermometer
rain	
snow	
cloud cover	
wind speed	
wind direction	

7 Measuring Air Pressure

Did you know that the weight of the air above you is pushing on you right now? Air pushing on you is called **air pressure.** We do not feel this pressure because our bodies are used to it.

Meteorologists have noticed that areas with different air pressures get different weather. For example, an area with low air pressure may get rain or snow. Areas with high air pressure usually get clear and sunny weather.

The instrument that is used to measure changes in the air pressure is called a **barometer** [buh-RAHM-ih-tuhr]. A barometer has two needles. The longer needle shows the air pressure right now. You move the shorter needle, called the set needle, to the same place as the long needle. When the air pressure rises or falls, the longer needle will move. The set needle stays where you put it. When you look at the barometer again later, you can tell whether the air pressure has risen (increased) or fallen (decreased). After each barometer reading you should move the set needle to where the other needle is.

Learning Tip

Pause and think. Ask yourself: What did I just read? What did it mean? Put the information into your own words.

Set needle

◀ A barometer measures air pressure. Has the air pressure shown on this barometer risen or fallen?

Make Your Own Barometer

Skills Focus: observing, measuring

1. Half fill a glass or jar with water. Add two drops of food colouring.

2. Put a clear plastic drinking straw in the water. Carefully suck on the straw until the water is halfway up. Pinch the straw at the top and seal the end with a piece of modelling clay.

3. Put a ruler in the jar beside the straw. Tape both the ruler and the straw to one side of the jar. Record the level of the water in the straw.

4. Make a table like the one below in your notebook.

Barometer

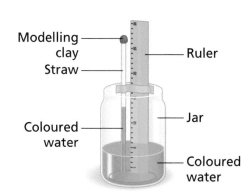

Date	Homemade barometer	School barometer

5. Check your homemade barometer once a day and record the level in the second column of your table. If the water level in the straw has gone up, the air pressure has increased. If it has gone down, the air pressure has decreased. Check the results from your homemade barometer against the school barometer. Record your reading from the school barometer in the third column.

⇨ Check Your Understanding

1. Draw and label three barometers to show
   - air pressure rising
   - air pressure falling
   - air pressure not changing

2. Add "air pressure" to your table and finish it.

8 Finding Weather Information

You can get information about the weather by making your own observations and measurements. You can also find weather information in the newspaper, on the radio, on TV, and on the Internet. Are there other places where you can find weather information?

Try This

Find Weather Information

Skills Focus: observing, communicating

1. Make a table like the one below.

Find Weather Information

Type of Information	Radio Station	TV Station	Newspaper	Telephone Service	Internet
Current temperature					
High temperature					
Low temperature					
Precipitation					
Cloud cover					
Wind direction					
Wind speed					
Air pressure					

2. Listen to a weather report on the radio. Record the name of the radio station on your table. Put a check mark in the square if the report provides that information.

3. Watch a weather report on a local TV station or The Weather Network. Record the name of the TV station on your table. Put a check mark in the square if the report provides that information.

4. Read the weather report in a newspaper. Record the name of the newspaper on your table. Put a check mark in the square if the report provides that information.

5. Check the blue pages in your phone book under Weather or under Environment Canada. There may be a number you can call to get current weather information and a weather forecast. Record the phone number on your table. Put a check mark in the square if the report provides that information.

6. Go to a weather Web site on the Internet. Record the name of the site on your table. Put a check mark in the square if the report provides that information.

www·science·nelson·com

⇨ Check Your Understanding

1. Did all the weather reports give you the same information? If not, what information was different?

2. Which weather report did you find the easiest to understand? Why?

3. If you wanted to know the temperature at lunchtime, which weather report would you use?

4. Why do you think weather information is available in so many different places?

Chapter Review

We can observe and measure the weather.

Key Idea: The air in our atmosphere can move and can hold water.

Vocabulary
weather p. 5
condensation p. 6
evaporation p. 6
water cycle p. 6
precipitation p. 7

Key Idea: We can use our senses to observe weather.

Key Idea: We can use instruments to measure weather.

Thermometer

Rain gauge

A few clouds

Cloudy

Cloud cover chart

Anemometer

Weather vane

Barometer

Vocabulary
temperature p. 10
thermometer p. 10
rain gauge p. 14
cloud p. 16
wind p. 20
wind speed p. 21
anemometer p. 21
wind direction p. 22
weather vane p. 22
air pressure p. 24
barometer p. 24

Key Idea: We can get weather information from many places.

Radio Station	TV Station	Newspaper	Telephone Service	Internet

Review Key Ideas and Vocabulary

Use the vocabulary words in your answers to the questions.

1. What two things can the air in our atmosphere do?

2. Describe how you could use each of your five senses to observe a windy, rainy day.

3. What do each of the following instruments measure?

Thermometer

Rain gauge

A few clouds

Cloudy

Cloud cover chart

Anemometer

Weather vane

Barometer

4. List at least three places where you can find information about today's weather.

Apply What You've Learned

Be a Meteorologist: Record and Report on the Weather

Looking Back

You have

- learned what meteorologists observe and measure when they study weather
- practised observing weather with your senses and measuring it with instruments
- made some of your own instruments
- read and listened to weather reports

In this activity, you will use what you have learned to measure and record information about the weather and make weather reports for your school.

Demonstrate Your Learning

Make a Weather Log

1. Make a table like the one on the next page.

2. Each day, at the same time, take readings and record the weather conditions.

Make a Local Weather Report

1. Each day, use the observations and measurements you recorded to write a weather report. Your teacher will choose one student to read his or her weather report for the class or the school.

Weather Log

Date						
Time						
Temperature—current						
Temperature—high						
Temperature—low						
Precipitation type						
Precipitation amount						
Cloud cover						
Wind speed						
Wind direction						
Air pressure						

⇨ Assessment Checklist

WEATHER LOG

As you observe, measure, and record the weather, make sure that you show you are able to

✔ measure accurately with weather instruments
✔ make realistic estimations of cloud cover
✔ record observations and measurements accurately
✔ communicate clearly
✔ work cooperatively with other students

LOCAL WEATHER REPORT

Your weather report should show that you are able to

✔ make an accurate report of current weather conditions
✔ use appropriate science words to describe weather
✔ communicate clearly

We can use patterns in weather to make weather predictions.

- ▸ We can find patterns in weather.
- ▸ Weather changes with the seasons.
- ▸ Different places have general weather patterns called climate.
- ▸ We can predict the weather.

Look at the photo above. What season do you think it is? Would you be surprised to know this photo was taken in June in North Vancouver? You already know a lot about weather patterns, so you know that snow is unusual in North Vancouver at this time of year.

Meteorologists use both observations and measurements to find weather patterns. They use these patterns to make the weather predictions you hear or read in weather forecasts.

Weather and the Seasons

▲ The seasons affect what this tree does. Do the seasons affect what you do?

What outdoor activities do you like to do in the summer?
Can you do these same activities in the winter? In British
Columbia, the weather in the summer is quite different from
the weather in the winter. These different weather
conditions affect our activities.

Weather Patterns and Activities

Skills Focus: interpreting data, inferring

→ Learning Tip

With a partner, look carefully at the seasonal calendar for Sachs Harbour. Look at one month at a time and list all the activities that happen during that month. Then move on to the next month.

The Inuvialuit [in-oo-vee-AL-oo-it] people in Sachs Harbour, in Canada's far north, have recorded their seasonal weather patterns and activities for scientists.

Seasonal Calendar for Sachs Harbour

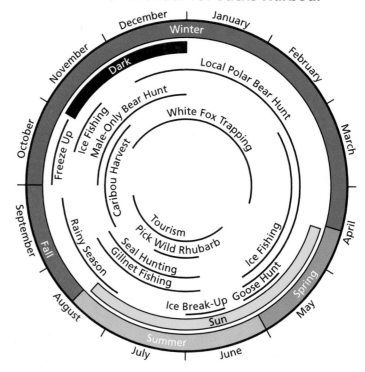

1. Which season is the longest in Sachs Harbour? Which season is the shortest?

2. What is the weather like in Sachs Harbour during the summer?

3. During what season do most people visit? What activities would they be able to see at that time?

What Causes Seasons?

The weather is different for each season because we live on a moving planet. Earth moves in two different ways. First, Earth spins. This spinning motion causes day and night. Second, Earth revolves around the Sun. It takes one whole year for Earth to go around the Sun.

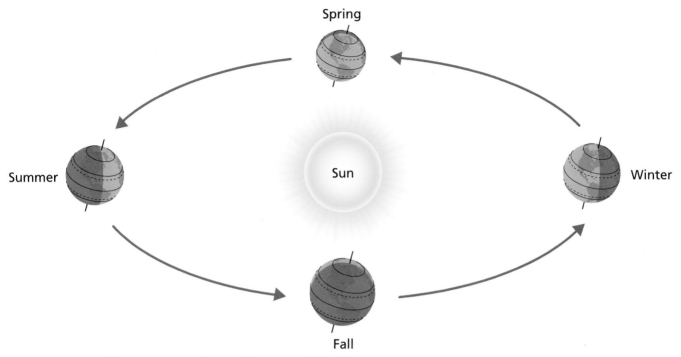

Seasons in the Northern Half of Earth

Spring

Summer

Sun

Winter

Fall

▲ The seasons change as Earth travels around the Sun.

Hours of Daylight

In summer, there are more hours of daylight in British Columbia. This means that the land gets more of the Sun's rays each day than in the winter. The added rays help to heat the land more in summer. In winter, there are fewer hours of daylight and the land gets less of the Sun's heat each day. So we have warmer weather in the summer and cooler weather in the winter.

Learning Tip

As you read ask yourself, "Why is this information important? How does it affect the weather?"

Check Your Understanding

1. Imagine your teacher tells you that new students will be arriving in your class from a country that has very different weather patterns. Working in a group, make a brochure to tell the new students what they might do outside in each season in your area. Illustrate your brochure with your own drawings or with pictures cut out of magazines.

2. How do the hours of daylight affect the heating of Earth?

The Effect of Mountains and Oceans on Our Climate

Meteorologists use averages of temperature and precipitation to describe general patterns. They call the general pattern of weather for an area its normal weather. Normal weather is also called **climate** [KLIE-mit]. The mountains and ocean affect the climate in British Columbia.

➡ Learning Tip

Set a purpose for your reading. Turn the two headings into questions, then read to answer them.

The Effect of Mountains on Precipitation

Mountains affect the amount of precipitation an area receives. Weather usually moves from west to east. Because British Columbia is beside the Pacific Ocean, the air picks up moisture from the ocean as it moves to the land. As air moves up over mountains, it cools and clouds form. Rain or snow falls. By the time the air has moved past the mountains, it has lost most of its moisture, so places on the east side of the mountains get very little precipitation.

Clouds form
and precipitation falls

Air rises
and cools

Drier and
warmer air

Moist air from
the ocean

▲ The mountains can cause rain or snow to fall. After the air moves over a mountain, the air is drier.

The Effect of Oceans on Temperature

As you travel farther north, the average temperature usually drops and the weather gets cooler. This is not always true in British Columbia.

How close an ocean is to a place affects the temperature. You already know that the Sun heats Earth. It takes more heat to raise the temperature of water than the temperature of land. In the summer, the land heats up more than the water. The cooler ocean water keeps the temperature of the land near it cooler than areas away from the ocean. So if you live in Vancouver, close to the water, and your friend lives in Abbotsford, which is inland away from the water, it will be cooler in the summer where you live.

Water also releases more heat than land does when it cools down. In the winter, the ocean will hold onto heat longer than land will, and this helps keep the temperatures of the areas around the water higher. So temperatures on the coast will be higher in winter than temperatures inland.

▲ Trail has much colder winters than Vancouver although it isn't farther north. What makes Vancouver winters warmer?

⇨ Check Your Understanding

1. What do meteorologists use to describe the climate of an area?

2. Why does one side of the mountains get more rain than the other?

3. Why does a wind from the ocean cool you on a hot summer day?

Weather Patterns in Different Places

Kamloops and Prince Rupert are two cities in British Columbia. Looking at the map, you can see that Prince Rupert is near the water and Kamloops is inland on the east side of the mountains.

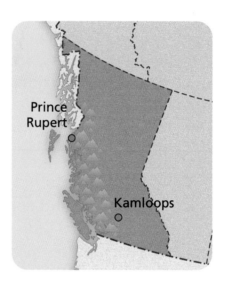

⇨ Learning Tip

When reading a graph with two lines or bars, ask yourself, "Why are there two lines or bars? What am I supposed to notice?"

Try This

Compare Climates

Skills Focus: interpreting data

1. Read the following graphs.

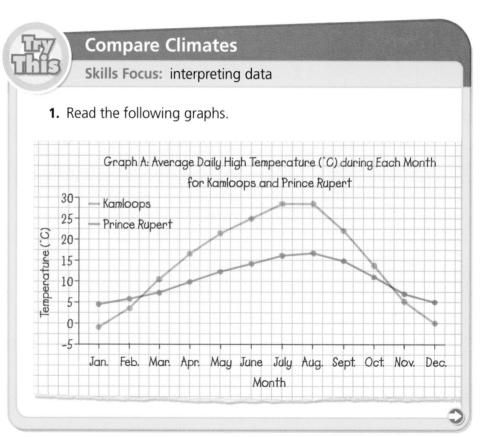

Graph A: Average Daily High Temperature (°C) during Each Month for Kamloops and Prince Rupert

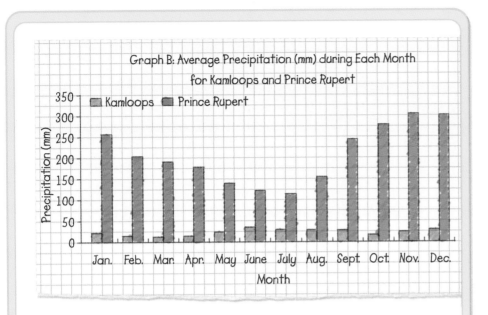

Graph B: Average Precipitation (mm) during Each Month for Kamloops and Prince Rupert

2. Which city gets the most precipitation?

3. Which city has the hottest temperatures?

4. Which city is hotter and drier?

5. Which city is cooler and wetter?

6. How does the area where you live compare to Prince Rupert and Kamloops? Is it more like one city than the other city?

7. Find out what the temperature and precipitation are like in your area.

www·science·nelson·com

⇨ **Learning Tip**

To find the average of a set of data, count how many numbers are in your data set. Add the numbers together. Divide the sum you get by how many numbers there are.

```
  16        18
  18     4)72
  21       -4
+ 17       32
  72      -32
           0
```

▲ If the daily high temperatures for four days were 16 °C, 18 °C, 21 °C, and 17 °C, then the average daily high temperature for those days would be 18 °C.

⇨ Check Your Understanding

1. If you like to snowboard in the winter, would Kamloops or Prince Rupert be the best place to live? Explain your answer.

4 Conduct an Investigation

SKILLS MENU

○ Questioning   ○ Classifying
● Predicting   ○ Inferring
○ Observing   ● Interpreting Data
● Measuring   ● Communicating

Heating Water and Land

In this investigation, you will work with a partner to make a model of water and land. You will use pans of water and sand to represent the ocean and the land. Then you will investigate how the water and land are heated by the Sun. You will use a lamp to represent the Sun.

cake pan

thermometer

sand   scoop

lamp   water

Question

Will the water or land be heated more by the Sun?

Prediction

Make a prediction about whether the water or sand will be heated more by the lamp.

Materials

- 2 small metal cake pans
- sand in a plastic container
- gooseneck lamp
- bulb thermometer
- plastic scoop
- water in a plastic drink jug

Procedure

Step 1 Put the water in one pan and the sand in the other pan. Make sure that there is about the same amount of water and sand.

Step 2 Take the temperature of the water and the sand. Record each temperature. The two temperatures should be about the same.

Step 3 Turn the lamp on and shine the light on the sand for 30 minutes. Turn the lamp off, then record the temperature of the sand. Turn the lamp on again and shine the light on the water for 30 minutes. Turn the lamp off and record the temperature of the water.

 Do not touch the light bulb as it could be very hot.

Step 4 Compare your results with another pair of students. Did you get similar changes in temperatures?

Interpret Data and Observations

1. Did the temperature of the water or the sand rise the most?

2. Was your prediction correct?

3. Predict what would happen if you left the light on each pan for one hour. What about for two hours? Ask your teacher if you can try this to see if your prediction is correct.

Apply and Extend

1. Many people like to go swimming on hot days. How do the results of this investigation help you explain this?

2. How do your results help you explain why Prince Rupert is warmer in winter and cooler in summer than Kamloops, even though Prince Rupert is farther north?

3. Revelstoke is in the mountains. Powell River is beside the ocean. Which do you think has cooler summers? How can you check your prediction?

⇨ Check Your Understanding

1. Why is it a good idea to do an investigation to check your predictions?

2. Why is it a good idea to compare your results with your classmates' results?

5 Using Air Pressure to Predict Weather

Some weather predictions are easy to make. For example, you can predict the kind of weather you will likely have during the different seasons where you live. It is more difficult to predict the weather for each day.

The weather forecasts we hear or read each day are predictions. Meteorologists make these weather predictions based on observations and measurements.

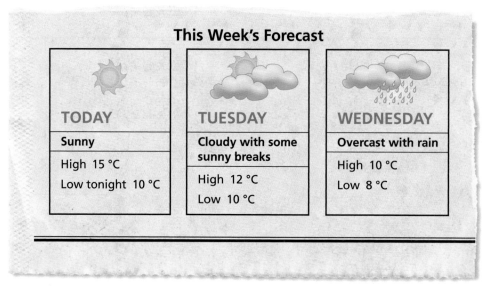

This Week's Forecast

TODAY	TUESDAY	WEDNESDAY
Sunny	**Cloudy with some sunny breaks**	**Overcast with rain**
High 15 °C	High 12 °C	High 10 °C
Low tonight 10 °C	Low 10 °C	Low 8 °C

▲ Look at this weather forecast from a newspaper. What day would you carry an umbrella?

> **Learning Tip**
>
> As you read, make connections to things you learned earlier. Ask yourself, "How does this fit with what I learned about measuring air pressure?"

Our day-to-day weather depends on the large bodies of air called air masses. To predict the weather, meteorologists look at the kinds of air masses moving across our area, and what the air is like in those air masses. Changes in air pressure give them important clues about the air masses that are coming our way. Chances are, if the air pressure changes, so will the weather.

Moving Air

Observe Moving Air

Skills Focus: observing, inferring, questioning

1. Work with a partner. Tape one plastic bag tightly to one end of a straw.

2. Blow into the straw to put some air into the bag. Make sure the bag is at least half-full of air.

3. Now quickly tape a second plastic bag to the other end of the straw.

4. Put one hand on one bag and your other hand on the other bag. Have fun pushing the air back and forth between the two bags.

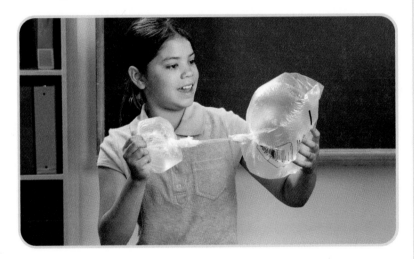

5. How can you keep an equal amount of air in each bag? What has to happen to move the air from one bag into the other bag?

6. Write two of your own questions about this activity. Trade your questions with a partner and try to answer each other's questions.

You can't see the air in the bags, but you can feel it. When you push on the air in one bag, you are increasing the air pressure in that bag. The air pressure in the other bag is lower, so some of the air moves into that bag. If you were standing inside the straw, what would you feel?

Moving Air and Air Pressure

Air always moves from higher pressure areas to lower pressure areas. Air pressure changes as weather systems move by. Like the air in the bags, we can't see air masses moving, but we can use our barometer to measure the changes in air pressure. We can also use our anemometer to measure the wind speed.

If the barometer shows us that air pressure is falling, we know a low pressure air mass is coming our way. Low pressure air masses sometimes bring clouds and precipitation. If our barometer shows us that air pressure is rising, we know a high pressure air mass is coming our way. High pressure air masses usually bring clear skies.

▲ Look at these photos of weather. What type of air pressure goes with each kind of weather?

⟡ Learning Tip

Reread the paragraph above to help you answer the question under the photos.

Tracking Air Masses

Weather forecasters use the information from several weather stations to make predictions. Weather forecasters use this information to help them make their own weather forecasts. If they see a high pressure area moving slowly toward them, they estimate how long it will take to arrive. They can then make a prediction about the weather.

1. We can't see air masses, so how can we tell they are moving?

2. Look at the barometers below. In each case, the red needle shows yesterday's air pressure. Predict if the weather will change, and in what way.

Today

Today

Today

3. How do weather forecasters use information from other places to help them make a forecast?

Chapter 2

6 Using Clouds to Predict Weather

→ Learning Tip

Before you read, scan the section and notice the highlighted words. What three types of clouds will you learn about?

Take a look at the sky. You will probably see some clouds. Clouds cover about half of Earth at any given time. Clouds are one of the best ways to predict what the weather will be like for the next little while.

Clouds are grouped by the way they look. There are only three main types of clouds, so it is easy to recognize them. You might see more than one type of cloud in the sky at one time.

Cumulus clouds [KYOOM-yuh-luhs kloudz] are fluffy-looking clouds. They are often tall clouds, piled high and puffy, like cotton puffs stacked together but with flat bottoms. Sometimes cumulus clouds are big and close to the ground, and sometimes they are high up in the air and look very tiny. Cumulus clouds usually mean that there will be fair weather. However, if they are very tall and have dark bottoms, they may bring thunderstorms.

▲ Cumulus clouds

Cirrus clouds [SEAR-uhs kloudz] are thin, feather-like clouds that can look like hair. They show the direction the wind is blowing. They are always very high in the sky and are made up of ice crystals. They can mean that there will be no precipitation now, but that a low pressure air mass is approaching. The low pressure air mass might bring rain or snow.

▲ Cirrus clouds

Stratus clouds are flat, layered clouds. They often block the Sun and cause a dull, grey day or bring rainy weather. Fog is a stratus cloud at ground level.

▲ Stratus clouds

Learning Tip

Close your eyes and try to "see" the type of cloud that would bring rain.

The colour of a cloud tells you how much water is in it. Very white clouds have little moisture. Very dark clouds have lots of moisture and will probably bring rain.

Start looking at clouds and you may begin to see some patterns. If you see dark stratus clouds coming, take an umbrella to school! If you see a few cumulus clouds in the sky, you can enjoy fair weather. If there are cirrus clouds in the sky, it may rain or snow tomorrow or the day after. You can even see clouds changing through the day. Look at the sky before school, and look at it again at different times during the day to see if there are any changes.

Check Your Understanding

1. Record the types of clouds you see over the next five days. Do this twice a day, once in the morning and once in the afternoon. Choose the same times each day.

Day	Day 1	Day 2	Day 3	Day 4
Type of Cloud	Morning: cumulus	Morning:	Morning:	Morning:
	Afternoon:	Afternoon:	Afternoon:	Afternoon:

2. Draw and label the three main types of clouds—cumulus, cirrus, and stratus.

3. What can each type of cloud tell you about the weather?

Tech·CONNECT

Weather Satellites

When you look into the sky, you see only a small piece of it. You can make weather predictions based on the clouds that you see. Imagine if you could see farther. Do you think you would make better predictions?

Weather satellites allow us to see much farther and make better predictions. Weather satellites take pictures of the clouds and send them to weather stations on the ground. These pictures help weather forecasters warn people about the changing weather that is on the way.

Because of weather satellites, forecasters can even see storms developing far out over the Pacific Ocean.

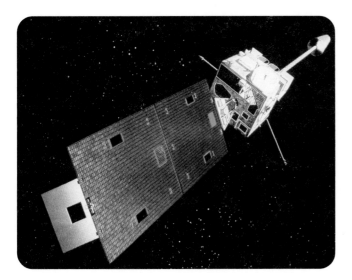

The photos below show a storm moving into the coast of British Columbia. Look at the time of each photograph. How could these photos help forecasters predict the weather?

▲ 3:00 a.m.

▲ 12:00 noon

You can watch satellite pictures of the atmosphere on your computer. You can even watch the same picture over a day to see how it changes.

www·science·nelson·com GO

Chapter Review

We can use patterns in weather to make weather predictions.

Key Idea: We can find patterns in weather.

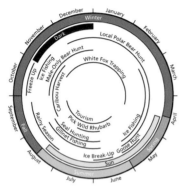

Seasons

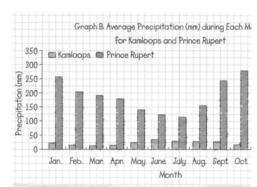

Graph B: Average Precipitation (mm) during Each Month for Kamloops and Prince Rupert

Climate

Key Idea: Weather changes with the seasons.

Spring

Summer

Fall

Winter

Key Idea: Different places have general weather patterns called climate.

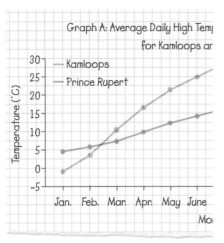
Temperature

Precipitation

Key Idea: We can predict the weather.

Changes in air pressure

Types of clouds

Review Key Ideas and Vocabulary

Use the vocabulary words in your answers to the questions.

1. What two types of patterns can we find in weather?

2. Why does weather change with the seasons?

3. What two things do meteorologists measure to determine an area's climate?

4. How does air pressure help meteorologists predict the weather? How does cloud type help them predict the weather?

Be a Meteorologist: Predict the Weather

Looking Back

You have learned

- about the patterns in weather—patterns caused by the seasons and by the climate of a particular place
- how air pressure and cloud type can be used to predict day-to-day weather

In this activity, you will record your observations and measurements of weather. You will use what you have learned about predicting weather to develop a weather forecast for your area.

Demonstrate Your Learning

Make a Local Weather Forecast

1. Work in a small group. Record your observations and measurements about weather in a weather log or on a class weather chart.

2. Make a forecast each day for five days. Use your observations and measurements and what you have learned about predicting weather. Your forecast should include predictions about
   - temperature
   - precipitation
   - wind

3. How accurate are your forecasts? Keep track of your success rate. What can you do to make your success rate better? How do your forecasts compare with forecasts you hear on the radio, see on television, or read in the newspaper?

4. Each day, your teacher will choose one group to make a public weather forecast. When it is your turn, decide how you want to present your forecast. You can do it
   - orally like a radio reporter
   - with charts and diagrams like a television reporter
   - with icons and words like in a newspaper

⇨ Assessment Checklist

LOCAL WEATHER FORECAST

Your weather forecasts for the next day should show that you are able to

✔ use air pressure and cloud type to predict the next day's weather
✔ make reasonable predictions about temperature, precipitation, and wind based on observations and measurements
✔ use appropriate science words to describe weather
✔ communicate clearly

Weather affects living and non-living things.

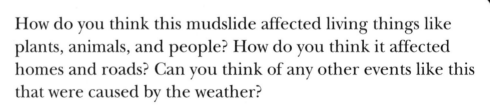

How do you think this mudslide affected living things like plants, animals, and people? How do you think it affected homes and roads? Can you think of any other events like this that were caused by the weather?

Begin a collection of weather articles from the newspaper. Some articles will be on the front page. Others will be inside the newspaper. Post the articles on a bulletin board in your classroom.

Weather Affects Non-Living Things

You know the weather affects you, but did you know that weather can break up rocks?

Freeze Water

Skills Focus: observing, communicating

1. Take a small plastic container with a snap lid, and fill it with water. Snap the lid in place, making sure that it is tightly closed to stop air from getting in the container. There should be little or no air in the container.

2. Put the container in a freezer and leave it overnight.

3. Describe what happens.

 Do not try this with a glass container.

In nature, water flows into little cracks and openings in rocks. When winter comes, the water may freeze because of low temperatures and break off pieces of rock.

▲ Water expands when it freezes. This can break off pieces of rock like the ones in this photo.

Moving Soil and Rocks

You have learned that weather can affect rocks. How does the weather affect other non-living things?

Make Rain on a Mountain

Skills Focus: predicting, observing

1. Work with a partner. Place some soil and small rocks in a large pan that has high sides. Mix the soil and rocks, and add enough water so the soil will stick together. Do not use too much water.

2. Pile the mixed soil and rocks into a small mountain. Pack it down a little. Draw a picture of your mountain.

3. Predict what will happen to the mountain when you pour water on top of it. Write your prediction in your notebook.

4. Fill a small watering can with water and slowly pour the water onto the top of the mountain. Observe what happens to the mountain.

5. Did some parts of the mountain wash away more easily than other parts? Draw a picture of the mountain after you have poured all the water on top of it.

The movement of rocks and soil from one place to another is called **erosion** [ih-ROW-zhun]. Erosion can happen very quickly or very slowly. During gentle rains, the water washes the soil away little by little. This happens so slowly that you may not even notice it. When there is a big rainstorm, the water can have a much greater effect on the land and on human-made things like roads. Flowing water in rivers slowly erodes the riverbanks. When the water flows quickly because of storms or floods, the water erodes the banks more quickly.

Even light, fluffy snowflakes cause erosion. When snow falls on a steep slope in the mountains, it forms a layer. As more snow falls during the winter, new layers are formed. Sometimes, a layer slides down the slope into the valley. We call this an avalanche. Avalanches can cause a lot of erosion in just a few seconds.

➡ **Learning Tip**

As you read this page, ask yourself, "How does this fit with what I already know?"

▲ Water erodes riverbanks.

▲ Avalanches erode mountainsides.

➡ Check Your Understanding

1. Suppose you made another, larger soil-and-rock mountain outside. Predict what would happen to your mountain if you left it in the rain for a month.

2. Where does the soil go when it is moved by erosion?

3. How can snow cause erosion?

2 Seasonal Weather Affects Living Things

→ Learning Tip

Before you read this section, fill in the "Know" column of a Know-Wonder-Learned chart about how weather affects plants and animals.

What do you do when it rains? How do you dress for the snow? How do you protect yourself from the Sun? Like you, all living things must be able to deal with changes in the weather. If they can't, they may not survive.

Animal needs include food, shelter, and warmth. Plant needs include water, nutrients from the soil, and sunlight to make their own food. Plants usually do not grow in temperatures below 0 °C.

The seasons bring many changes to the weather in British Columbia, and living things adapt to seasonal weather in many different ways. Adapt is just another word for change.

How Animals Adapt to the Seasons

Some animals migrate to a warmer place to stay for the winter. Many birds, such as Canada geese and rufous hummingbirds, migrate. Migrating birds travel thousands of kilometres each year as they fly south for the winter and then return to British Columbia for the summer.

▲ The winters in the Lower Mainland are so mild that geese stay all year. But in most parts of British Columbia, geese fly south for the winter.

Some animals hibernate through the winter. Hibernating is like sleeping. Before they begin to hibernate, the animals eat lots of food, which is stored as fat. As they hibernate, their bodies use this fat as a food source. When the animals come out of hibernation in the spring, they are very hungry! The ground squirrel and the hoary marmot are two animals that hibernate during the winter.

▲ A hibernating ground squirrel

Not all animals migrate or hibernate during the winter. Animals that stay active during the winter must find food and shelter. They must also stay warm. Animals that have fur often grow a thicker coat for the winter to help them stay warm. If you have a pet dog or cat, you may have noticed this. In the spring, these animals do not need the extra fur so they shed it. Other animals put on more fat, which helps to keep them warm. The fat is also a food source, which their bodies use during the winter.

▲ Some animals, like these mountain goats, grow extra fur to keep warm in the winter, then shed it in spring.

Some animals change the colour of their fur during the seasons. Some rabbits will grow brown fur in the summer and white fur in the winter. Rabbits with white fur are harder to see in the snow. Rabbits with brown fur are harder to see in dry grass and shrubs. This makes it harder for other animals to catch the rabbits, and easier for the rabbits to survive.

▲ Rabbits with white fur are hard to see in the snow. Rabbits with brown fur are hard to see in grass and shrubs.

How Plants Adapt to the Seasons

Plants also adapt to seasonal changes in the weather. Some plants live for only one growing season. During the growing season, they grow from seeds, and produce flowers with seeds for the next year. They die when the winter comes. The next spring, the seeds sprout to produce new plants.

Other plants grow for more than one year, but many are dormant in the winter. Dormant means they do not grow. Trees that lose their leaves in the fall are dormant during the winter. When the spring comes, they produce new leaves and begin to grow again.

Spring

Winter

▲ This lilac bush grows in the spring, but it is dormant in the winter.

⇨ Check Your Understanding

1. How does the weather affect the activities that you do in each season?

2. What are some activities that you can do no matter what the weather is like?

3. Name four different ways that animals adapt to seasonal changes in the weather.

4. What happens to animals that cannot adapt to changing seasonal weather conditions?

5. Name two ways that plants adapt to seasonal changes in the weather.

Winter Weather Affects British Columbians

→ Learning Tip

As you read, make connections to your own life. Which photo of winter is most like the winter where you live?

What is winter weather like where you live? Winter weather is not the same all over British Columbia. Some parts of the province receive a lot of rain in winter. Other parts receive a lot of snow. Other parts receive less snow but more cold weather.

▲ Winter weather brings rain in the Lower Mainland, snow in the North Coast, and cold and wind in the North East.

Rainy Weather

People who live in the Lower Mainland and on the coast of Vancouver Island have rainy winters. They use umbrellas and wear outdoor clothing made of fabrics that do not get wet easily. Fabrics that do not get wet easily are called water resistant.

▲ This modern rain jacket and this traditional cedar blanket are both water resistant.

Test Fabrics for Water Resistance

Skills Focus: predicting, observing, interpreting data

1. Arrange small squares of fabric in a row on a piece of coloured construction paper. Some fabrics you can use are fleece, cotton, nylon, plastic, wool, and Gore-Tex. Print the names of the fabrics above the squares. Predict which fabric will be the most water resistant, and label it "1" beside its name. Predict which fabric will be the next most water resistant, and label it "2." Continue until you have ranked all the pieces.

2. Below the row of squares, print the word "Results."

3. Spray "rain" on the squares of fabric using a plastic squirt bottle. Try to spread the "rain" evenly.

4. Lift the squares to see how much water soaked through to the construction paper for each piece of fabric. Label the driest square "1," the second driest square "2," continuing until all the squares are ranked.

5. Compare the results with your predictions. Were your predictions correct?

Heavy Snowfall

Snow can be very different across parts of British Columbia. The mountains can get huge amounts of snow each winter. Snow on the northern coastal mountains is often wet and heavy, so people have to wear waterproof boots. Snow in the interior is often dry and fluffy. Snowshoes help people walk in very deep snow.

In places that get a lot of snow, homes and buildings are built in special ways so the snow cannot damage them. One of the special ways is the design of the roof.

Cold and Snowy Weather

The interior and northern plains of British Columbia get less snow than on the coast, but they are much colder. People have to wear warm winter clothes that prevent their bodies from losing heat to the atmosphere. Inuit [IN-oo-iht] people invented hooded jackets called parkas. The Inuit made parkas out of animal hides because those materials are good at keeping body heat from being lost to the atmosphere.

▲ Snowshoes were invented by Aboriginal peoples. They help people walk in deep snow without sinking in too far.

▲ What will happen to the snow as it falls on this roof?

▲ These girls from Holman Island, NWT, wear parkas to stay warm.

In the following activity, you will try to insulate an ice cube to slow down its melting. Your teacher will provide you with a variety of materials to use.

Insulate an Ice Cube

Skills Focus: predicting, observing, interpreting data

1. Wrap an ice cube in the material you think will best insulate it.

2. Leave the ice cube sitting on your desk for one hour.

3. Then open it up and see how much of the ice cube has melted.

4. Compare your results with those of your classmates. Which materials did the best job of insulating the ice cube?

⇨ Check Your Understanding

1. Describe the winter weather where you live. Draw and label a picture of yourself to show things you do to deal with the effects of this weather.

2. Suppose that you were going to build a cabin in a place that receives a large amount of snow each winter. Look at the three pictures of cabins below. Which roof design would you choose? Why?

3. Many Aboriginal peoples have lived in the same area for hundreds or thousands of years. What might scientists be able to learn about the effects of weather from these Aboriginal peoples?

Extreme Weather Events Affect Living and Non-Living Things

Have you ever experienced an extreme weather event like a thunderstorm or a heavy snowfall? Extreme weather events can have extreme effects on both living and non-living things.

Thunderstorms

When you hear a sharp crack of thunder and see lightning, you are near a thunderstorm. If you hear a thunderstorm you should go indoors. If you are safe, thunderstorms can be spectacular! As well as thunder and lightning, thunderstorms can have strong winds and heavy rain. Thunderstorms can also cause flooding, and lightning can start forest fires.

▲ This fire, in the Kelowna area, was started by lightning.

▲ Crouch down if you are outdoors during a thunderstorm. Do not stand under trees.

Hail

Sometimes thunderstorms bring hail. Hail can damage crops in farmers' fields and plants in gardens. It can also break windows and damage cars.

▲ Hailstones

Did you know?

The heaviest hailstone to fall in Canada weighed 290 g. It fell in Saskatchewan in 1973. The heaviest hailstone ever recorded fell in China in 1995. It weighed 15 kg!

Tornadoes

Sometimes a thunderstorm can create a tornado. Tornadoes, which are also called twisters, do not happen very often in British Columbia. A tornado is a funnel-shaped storm that spins quickly. The winds in a tornado can be as high as 500 km/h. Tornadoes can destroy buildings and crops. Fortunately, tornadoes are not very big, so the damage is limited to a small area.

▲ A tornado

▲ Tornado damage to houses

Blizzards

A blizzard is a snowstorm that has very high winds. These winds blow the snow, which makes it hard to see outside. The blowing snow also makes large snow piles. The winds make the temperature seem much colder than it really is. This is called wind chill. Blizzards can happen in the interior of British Columbia, but are not common along the coast.

▲ Blowing snow from a blizzard makes it very hard to see.

Drought

A long time without rain is called a drought [DROUT]. We might be able to water our gardens, but it is harder for farmers to water their crops. The lack of water is also hard on wild plants and animals.

▲ The effects of drought on a corn crop

1. Make a table like the one below in your notebook.

	Extreme Weather Event	Effects on Living Things	Effects on Non-Living Things
	Thunderstorm		

- In the first column, list the extreme weather events you learned about in this section. You can add another extreme weather event you know about if you like.
- Draw a picture of each extreme weather event under its name.
- Work with a small group to discuss how each extreme weather event might affect living things (wild plants, wild animals, pets, gardens and crops, people) and non-living things (hillsides, rivers, buildings). Use some examples from the textbook, then try to think of some other examples. Use drawings and words to explain these effects in the second and third columns of your table.

2. What extreme weather events have you experienced? How did they affect you?

ScienceWorks

The UV Index: A Canadian Success Story

Have you ever had a sunburn? You got the sunburn because you were exposed to harmful ultraviolet (UV) rays from the Sun.

Scientists have been studying the effects of UV rays on humans for many years. They have discovered that UV rays can be harmful to your health by causing skin cancer, problems with eyesight, and problems with your body's ability to fight disease. Everybody's skin is different, so some people will burn faster than others. Protecting yourself from UV rays is important.

In 1992, Canadian scientists invented the UV Index. The UV Index is an easy way to tell how strong the Sun's UV rays are. It is a simple scale and is easy to use—the higher the number, the stronger the rays. In 1994, the UV Index was adopted throughout the world as the best way to inform people about the possible risks to their health from UV rays.

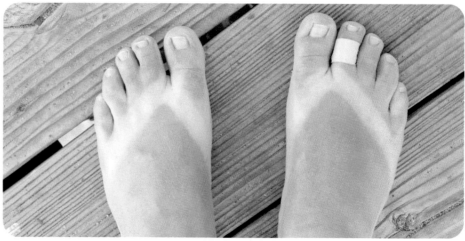

▲ Sunburns can be very painful.

UV Index	Category	Time to affect your health	What you can do
Over 9	Extreme	Less than 15 minutes	• If possible, stay out of the sun. • If you go outside, wear clothes that cover your body, a hat, and sunglasses. Use sunscreen of at least 15 SPF. Stay in the shade. • Don't stay outside very long.
7–9	High	Less than 20 minutes	• Use a sunscreen of at least 15 SPF. • Stay out of the sun between 10:00 a.m. and 4:00 p.m. • Wear a hat, sunglasses, and clothes that cover your body.
4–7	Moderate	About 30 minutes	• Stay in the shade during the middle of the day. • If you burn easily, use sunscreen and wear sunglasses and clothes that cover your body.
0–4	Low	More than one hour	• Wear sunglasses on bright days. • If you burn easily, use sunscreen and wear clothes that cover your body.

In 1998, a meteorologist named Angus Fergusson started the Children's UV Index Sun Awareness Program. This program encourages children to learn about UV rays and Sun safety.

Chapter Review

Weather affects living and non-living things.

Key Idea: Weather affects non-living things.

Examples of erosion

Key Idea: Weather affects the growth and behaviour of living things.

Growth

Behaviour

Key Idea: Extreme weather events affect living and non-living things.

Thunderstorm

Hail

Tornado

Blizzard

Drought

Review Key Ideas and Vocabulary

Use the vocabulary words in your answers to the questions.

1. Draw and label diagrams to explain how rain can cause erosion.

2. Make a poster of a winter scene that shows how plants and animals, including people, adapt to winter weather conditions.

3. Draw a picture of an extreme weather event in the middle of your page. Use pictures and words to make a web describing how it can affect living and non-living things.

Apply What You've Learned

Research and Write a Weather Article

Looking Back

You have learned

- how weather can affect living and non-living things
- about the effects of seasonal weather changes and extreme weather events

In this activity, you will choose one of the things you have learned about and do research to learn more about it. Then you will use the information to write an article about your topic.

Demonstrate Your Learning

Do Research

1. **Choose a topic** Choose something in this chapter about the effects of weather that you found really interesting, or that you would like to know more about.

2. **Check your topic** Check your topic with your teacher.

3. **Identify the information you need** Identify what you already know about the topic. Identify what you don't know. Make a list of key questions that you need to answer.

4. **Find sources of information** Identify all the places where you could look for information on your topic. These might include books, videotapes, people in your community, and Internet sites.

5. **Evaluate the sources of information** Look over your information sources and decide whether they are useful. Does each source of information make sense to someone your age?

6. **Record and organize the information** Identify categories or headings for note-taking. You may want to use these to develop a table for note-taking. Record information in your own words, perhaps in point form.

Write a Weather Article

1. Use the information you collected to write an article about your weather topic. Use drawings to help explain the information and to make your article more interesting.

⇨ Assessment Checklist

RESEARCH

As you look for and record information, make sure that you show you are able to

- ✔ identify appropriate sources of information
- ✔ choose useful information
- ✔ record information in your own words
- ✔ organize information

WEATHER ARTICLE

Your weather article should show that you are able to

- ✔ include accurate facts
- ✔ use appropriate science words to describe weather
- ✔ use illustrations to explain ideas
- ✔ communicate clearly

Making Connections

Make a Weather Channel Broadcast

Looking Back

In this unit, you have learned

- how to observe and measure the weather in order to make weather reports
- how to predict the weather to make weather forecasts
- about the effects of weather and written a weather article

Now your class is ready to do a weather channel broadcast!

Demonstrate Your Learning

If you have cable or satellite television, you might have watched the weather channel. This TV channel shows only weather information.

1. Watch the weather channel for 30 minutes or so. You will notice that the format is usually weather report, weather forecast, weather story. Follow this format when you do your broadcast.

2. Work in a group. One person should do a current weather report, another person do a current weather forecast, then a third person read the weather article he or she wrote at the end of Chapter 3.

3. Your teacher will give each group a turn to participate. If possible, videotape your broadcast to show other classes or your parents.

⇨ Assessment Checklist

WEATHER REPORT
Your weather report should show that you are able to

- ✔ make accurate observations and measurements about weather
- ✔ record observations and measurements accurately
- ✔ make an accurate report of current weather conditions
- ✔ use appropriate science words to describe weather
- ✔ communicate clearly

WEATHER FORECAST
Your weather forecast should show that you are able to

- ✔ use air pressure and cloud type to predict weather
- ✔ make reasonable predictions about temperature, precipitation, and wind based on data
- ✔ use appropriate science words to describe weather
- ✔ communicate clearly

WEATHER ARTICLE
Your weather article should show that you are able to

- ✔ include accurate facts
- ✔ use appropriate science words to describe weather
- ✔ use illustrations to explain ideas
- ✔ communicate clearly

Preview

It's Canada Day and you have spent part of the day in the park with your friends and family. Many activities are going on in the park. A magician has been performing tricks, someone has been painting faces, and a band is playing. Now the Sun has set, and the sky is dark. Everyone looks up to see the fireworks. There is a whistling sound and then a booming sound. The sky is lit up with so many colours and shapes.

You see light and hear sounds every day. But do you know what light and sound are? Do you know where they come from? Are there other things about light and sound that you would like to find out? How will you find the answers?

In this unit, you will learn about light and sound. You will learn where light comes from and what it can do. You will also learn how sound is made and the different ways sound can behave.

 Observe Mini-Fireworks

Skills Focus: observing

1. Cover a 40 cm × 40 cm area of your desk with aluminum foil. Put a lump of modelling clay in the centre of the foil.

2. Darken your classroom. Stick a birthday sparkler in the modelling clay. Your teacher will light the sparkler. What can you see? What can you hear?

 Do not touch the sparkler while it is burning. Be careful that the sparks do not land on clothes, paper, or anything else that will burn. Do not touch the sparkler until it has completely cooled down.

◀ A fireworks display in Vancouver

There are many sources of light.

Key Ideas

- Light is a form of energy.
- Some light sources are natural.
- Some light sources are artificial.

 Never look directly at the Sun, even during an eclipse. It can permanently damage your eyes.

Have you ever seen a solar eclipse [ih-KLIPS]? When an eclipse occurs, the Moon blocks most of the light from the Sun and it gets very dark. When it gets dark in the day or night, we can turn on a light to see. Can you imagine what life would be like without light? Imagine if the Sun suddenly went black.

You use light every day, but do you know what light is? How do we produce light? Where does it come from? In this chapter, you will learn about light sources found in nature and light sources made by people. Light sources are things that make light.

What Is Light?

We need light to do many of our daily activities. But what is light? To understand what light is, we need to know what energy is. Scientists call the ability to do work **energy.**

Light is energy that we can see. Energy can change from one form to another. The following activity shows how light energy can change to heat energy and do work.

▲ What sources of light do you use in your classroom?

 Try This

Use Light Energy to Boil a Water Drop

Skills Focus: observing, inferring, recording

1. Place two pennies about 2 cm apart on a sidewalk in the sunlight.
2. Place a small drop of water on each penny.
3. Use a magnifying glass to focus a dot of sunlight on one of the drops. Keep the dot focused on the drop for a minute.

 Do not focus the magnifying glass on anything except the water drop.

4. Observe any differences between the water drops on the two pennies.

 The pennies may be hot. Do not pick them up until they cool.

Check Your Understanding

1. What can energy do?
2. How do you know light is a form of energy?

2 Natural Light

Before you read, look at the photos in this section. How many of these sources of light have you seen?

Light that comes from nature is called **natural** light. There are few natural light sources in the world. The Sun is our main source of natural light. The Sun both lights and warms our world. Life on Earth could not exist without the Sun.

Did you know that the Sun is a star? The other stars we see in the night sky are so far away we get very little light and heat from them.

▲ Stars are sources of natural light.

The Moon sometimes helps us to see at night. However, the Moon does not produce light. What we call moonlight is really just sunlight. The Moon shines because sunlight bounces off it.

▲ The Moon shining at night.

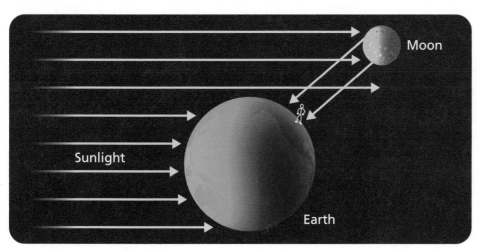

▲ Sunlight bounces off the Moon, making moonlight.

⇨ **Learning Tip**

Check your understanding of this diagram by explaining it to a partner.

Natural light is also produced by the northern lights, lightning, volcanoes, falling meteors [MEE-tee-uhrz], and forest fires.

▲ Some sources of natural light include the northern lights, lightning, volcanoes, and falling meteors.

Some living things, such as some animals and some mushrooms, can produce light.

▲ These mushrooms can produce natural light.

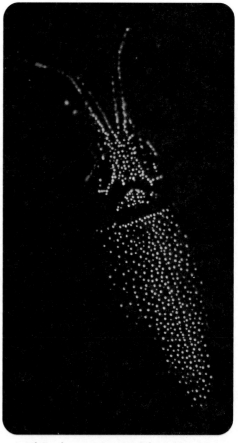

▲ This deep-sea squid can produce natural light.

Natural sources of light are important to us. However, we can't control them. For example, we can't turn the Sun on and off to meet our needs.

⇨ Check Your Understanding

1. What is the main source of natural light on Earth?
2. Write down three sources of natural light that you have seen. Write down one source of natural light that you know about, but have not seen.
3. What is moonlight?

Awesome SCIENCE

Creatures That Glow!

Imagine being able to make your own light using your body! Fireflies, some jellyfish, some mushrooms, and other creatures can produce their own light. Scientists call the ability of living things to create their own light bioluminescence [BY-oh-LOO-muh-NESS-uhns].

Different creatures use the light they produce in different ways. Some animals use bioluminescence to communicate. Female fireflies use flashes of light to attract male fireflies.

Some animals use light to escape from other animals that hunt them. For example, some squid produce glowing clouds to confuse animals that are attacking them. This allows the squid to escape. Some tiny sea creatures use flashes of light to scare animals that are hunting them. Any movement in the water will make these tiny creatures light up. They are often seen as a glow in the water behind a ship or a kayak [KIE-ak]. Even a hand moving in the water will make them light up.

▲ Fireflies use bioluminescence to communicate.

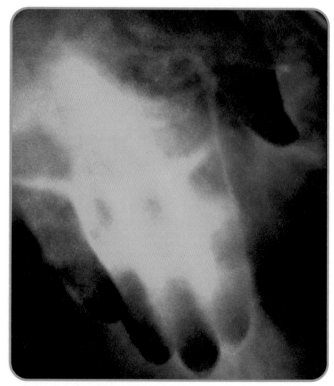

▲ Tiny sea creatures glow as a hand moves through the water.

Some animals use bioluminescence to hunt for food. An anglerfish has a glowing lure attached near its mouth. Small fish are attracted to the glow. Once the small fish gets close enough, the anglerfish attacks!

There are not many creatures on land that produce their own light, but bioluminescence is common in the deep ocean. In the deepest and darkest parts of the ocean, more than 90% of the animals have bioluminescence.

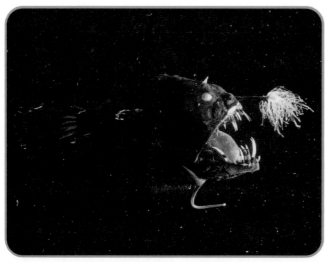

▲ An anglerfish uses a bioluminescent lure to get food.

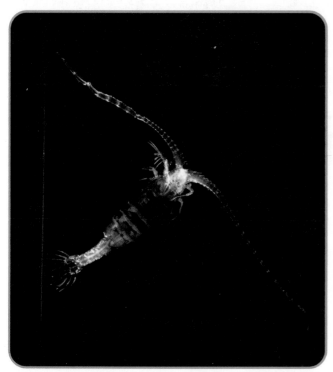

▲ Small swimming animals use bioluminescence to find each other.

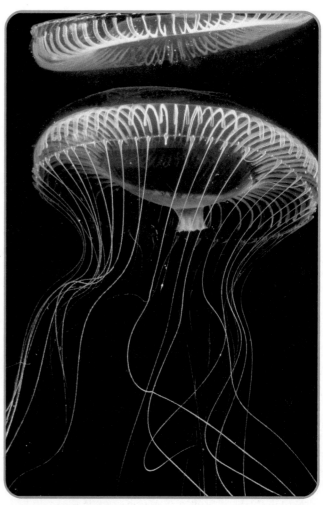

▲ Jellyfish use bioluminescence to attract small animals for food.

Artificial Light

A long time ago, the only sources of light that humans had were natural sources, such as the Sun. How different would your life be if the Sun was your only source of light? Once the Sun set, there would be almost no light, so you would probably just go to bed!

Over time, humans learned to control some natural light sources, and to make their own light sources. The first light source that humans learned to control was fire. They learned how to make fire to keep warm and cook with. Humans also used fire as a light source so that they could do things after the Sun went down.

Learning Tip

Study the photo carefully. How many light sources are there?

▲ Humans sometimes still use fire as a light source.

People learned that they could burn things other than wood to make light. Candles burn wax, oil lamps burn oil, and sparklers burn chemicals to produce light.

▲ Candle

▲ Oil lamp

▲ Sparklers

Any light that humans produce is called **artificial** [AR-tuh-FISH-uhl] light. Most artificial light is produced by electricity, which is another form of energy. These light sources are easy to control as they can be turned on and off by using a switch.

▲ Different kinds of light bulbs powered by electricity do many jobs for us.

Some natural light, like moonlight, bounces into our eyes from other sources. We also use artificial light bounced from other sources. For example, we can see road signs at night because light from car headlights or streetlights bounces off the road sign.

▲ Road signs bounce the light from car headlights to our eyes.

Natural light, like sunlight, is free. Artificial light always costs money. We pay for a lamp as well as the electricity or oil to make it work. We buy the flashlight and the batteries to make the flashlight work. We buy candles, sparklers, and reflective clothing. To save money and conserve energy, we shut off artificial lights when we are not using them.

⭢ **Learning Tip**

Locate the information you need to answer the questions by scanning the photos in the section.

⭢ **Check Your Understanding**

1. What kind of light do humans make?
2. List five sources of artificial light that you and your family use.
3. If the electricity went off tonight, what sources of artificial light could you use?

Tech·CONNECT

Edulight—A Canadian Invention

In many parts of the world there is a lot of sunlight during the day. However, many of these areas have no electricity for lights at night. With no artificial light, school children can't practise their reading after the Sun goes down. A Canadian invention called the Edulight is helping to change that. The Edulight is a small, solar-powered reading light.

◀ An Edulight

The light is called an Edulight because its inventors hope that it will help children get an education. In countries in Africa, such as Kenya, Ghana, Nigeria, and South Africa, many people use candles and paraffin lamps for light once the Sun sets.

Trying to read using these light sources is difficult because they do not create enough light. The makers of the Edulight have sent it to countries without electricity to promote reading.

▲ It is difficult to read by the light of a paraffin lamp.

The Edulight uses bright white LEDs (light emitting diodes) as its light source. LEDs don't burn out the way that normal light bulbs do. The Edulight has solar panels and rechargeable batteries instead of an electrical cord. The solar panels collect energy from the Sun, change it to electricity, and charge the batteries. The batteries are charged on sunny days, and after seven hours of sunlight will provide six hours of light.

This Canadian technology will bring reliable artificial light to children who could not otherwise read at night.

Chapter Review

There are many sources of light.

Key Idea: **Light is a form of energy.**

Vocabulary
energy p. 81

Key Idea: **Some light sources are natural.**

Vocabulary
natural p. 82

  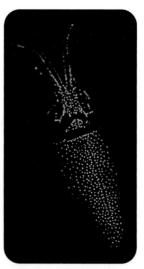

NEL

Key Idea: Some light sources are artificial.

Vocabulary
artificial p. 89

Review Key Ideas and Vocabulary

Use the vocabulary words in your answers to the questions.

1. What is light?

2. What is the difference between natural and artificial light?

3. Copy the following table in your notebook. Write two or more sources of light in each column. Some sources of light may be repeated in different columns.

Sources of Light					
Natural light			Artificial light		
Home	School	Community	Home	School	Community

Apply What You've Learned

Identify and Classify Sources of Light in Your World

Looking Back

You have learned

- that light is a form of energy we can see
- that there are natural light sources
- that there are artificial light sources

In this activity, you will use what you have learned to make a poster of natural and artificial light sources.

Demonstrate Your Learning

Make a Poster

1. Work with a partner or small group to brainstorm a list of light sources. You should have at least 10 examples in your list. Think about light sources that
   - occur in nature where you live
   - you use at home and at school
   - occur in your community

2. In your notebook, make a two-column table like the one below. Look at your list and decide whether each light source is natural or artificial. Write each example in the correct column in your table.

Natural light	Artificial light

3. Go through your list and draw a picture of each example, or find a picture to cut out of a magazine or newspaper flyer. Be sure to have your teacher's or your parent's permission before cutting up any magazines.

4. Divide a large piece of poster paper in half. Label one half of the paper "Natural light" and the other half "Artificial light." Paste your pictures and drawings in the correct area to make a display of your learning.

⇨ Assessment Checklist

POSTER

As you make your poster, make sure that you show you are able to

- ✔ work cooperatively with other students by sharing tasks
- ✔ communicate clearly by asking questions and making suggestions. If you disagree with something, discuss it with the others.
- ✔ identify light sources in nature, at home, at school, and in your community
- ✔ classify light sources as natural or artificial

Chapter 5

We can observe the properties of light.

Key Ideas

▸ Light travels in a straight line.

▸ Materials can be classified as transparent, translucent, or opaque.

▸ Materials can transmit, reflect, or absorb light.

▸ Our eyes can see light.

▸ Light can be refracted.

▸ Light can be separated into colours.

Rainbows are one of the most amazing sights on Earth. Do you know how a rainbow is made? Rainbows can be seen during a rain shower, but only when the Sun is out. What is it about light that makes a rainbow possible? Why can we suddenly see so many colours in the sky?

In this chapter, you will learn about the properties of light. You will learn how light is affected by different materials and how colour is a property of light.

Light Travels in a Straight Line

▲ Beams of sunlight travel in straight lines.

▲ Why is there a shadow here?

Have you ever seen beams of sunlight streaming down through the clouds? A **light beam** is made up of many light rays. A thin line of light energy is called a light ray. Light beams and light rays always travel in straight lines. This explains why shadows form behind objects. Shadows form when an object blocks a light beam.

Observe How Light Travels

Skills Focus: observing, measuring, inferring

1. On four index cards, draw lines from corner to corner to make an X. Make a hole at the centre of the X with a hole punch.

For a review on measuring length, see the Skills Handbook, page 228.

2. Stand the index cards up on a table using small lumps of modelling clay. Place the cards about 10 cm apart and try to make sure the holes are in a straight line.

3. Put a flashlight 10 cm from the first card. Turn on the flashlight. If needed, put the flashlight on a book to make sure the light goes through the holes.

4. Ask your teacher to darken your classroom. Can you see the light coming through the last hole? If not, adjust your cards. What does the light beam look like? Spray a fine mist of water along the light beam to make it show up better.

5. Move one card out of line. Can you still see the light shining through the last card? Explain what you see to a partner.

Before clocks were invented, people used shadows to tell the time. Sundials are made of an arm that casts a shadow on a base. Times are labelled around the base. As Earth spins, the Sun appears to travel across the sky. The shadow made by the arm of the sundial moves as the position of the Sun in the sky changes.

Offer opinions about what you have read. Do you think sundials have any advantages over modern clocks? Compare your opinion with a partner.

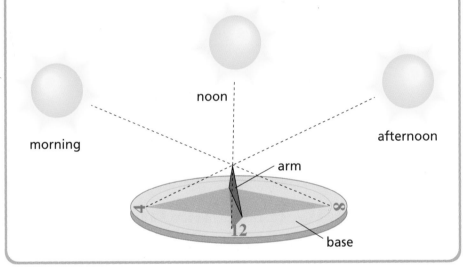

noon

morning

afternoon

arm

base

Check Your Understanding

1. In what type of path does light travel?

2. Why do you see shadows?

3. Why are there no shadows on faces when we take a picture using a camera flash?

Light Behaves in Different Ways in Different Materials

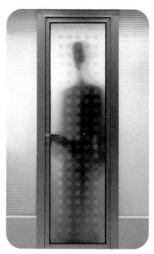

▲ What happens to light when it reaches each of these doors?

Some materials let light pass right through. We say that these materials **transmit** light. Which of the doors shown above can transmit light?

Transparent, Translucent, Opaque

⇨ Learning Tip

Use the photos to help you remember new words. Identify the correct vocabulary word for each door.

Materials that you can see clearly through because they transmit light are called **transparent** [trans-PAIR-uhnt]. Water and air are transparent. Clear glass and coloured cellophane are also transparent. Transparent materials are used for things that you can see through, such as windows and sandwich bags. Which door is transparent?

Materials that transmit some light but that you cannot see objects clearly through are called **translucent** [trans-LOO-sunt]. Frosted glass and plastic milk containers are translucent. Which door is translucent?

Materials that transmit no light are called **opaque** [oh-PAKE]. Opaque objects block all light and create shadows. Cement and wood are opaque. Many fabrics are also opaque. Blue jeans and fleece jackets are opaque. Which door is opaque?

▲ What items or parts of these items would you want to be opaque, translucent, or transparent and why?

Classify Materials

Skills Focus: observing, classifying, communicating

1. Look at the materials provided by your teacher. Decide whether they are transparent, translucent, or opaque.

2. In your notebook, make a table like the one below. Write or draw your findings in your table.

3. With a partner, think of two more transparent objects, two more translucent objects, and two more opaque objects. Write or draw these in your table.

Transparent	Translucent	Opaque

Reflecting and Absorbing Light

Transparent and translucent materials transmit most of the light that strikes them, but not all of it. Light can also **reflect** off these materials. When light reflects, it is bouncing off something. Windows transmit most of the light that strikes them, but they also reflect light. If you have a lamp turned on near a window at night, you can see the reflection of the lamp in the window.

Transparent and translucent materials also **absorb** some of the light that strikes them. When something absorbs light, it is soaking up the light. When light is absorbed by an object, the light energy changes to heat energy and the object heats up. If you touch a window that has been in the sunlight, you will notice that it is warm.

Opaque materials do not transmit any light. All of the light that strikes an opaque material is reflected or absorbed.

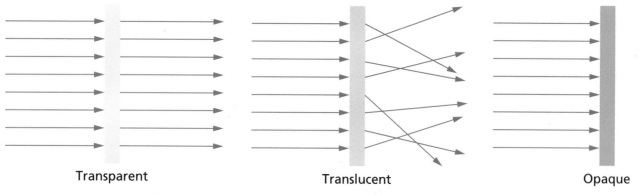

Transparent

Translucent

Opaque

▲ Transparent materials transmit most of the light that hits them. We can see straight through transparent materials.

▲ Translucent materials transmit most light, but they also cause light to bend. This makes objects seen through translucent materials look fuzzy.

▲ Opaque materials do not transmit any light. We can't see through opaque materials.

If a material is a light colour or has a smooth surface, more light will be reflected. Shiny opaque materials, such as mirrors, reflect most of the light that strikes them. If a material is a dark colour or has a rough surface, more light will be absorbed. Opaque objects that absorb light also become warm.

▲ Which of these surfaces will reflect more light? Which will absorb more light?

⇨ Check Your Understanding

1. Decide whether you would use a transparent, translucent, or opaque material in each of these cases. Explain your answer.
   - a living room window
   - a bathroom window
   - an envelope
   - a bathroom door
   - a sculpture

2. Look at the photo of the T-shirts above. Which T-shirt would you wear to stay cooler on a hot sunny day? Explain your answer.

3 Reflected Light

▶ Moonlight reflected off water is sunlight that has been reflected twice.

We can see things that produce light. We can see stars, fires, light bulbs, and fireflies. We can also see things that reflect light. When light is reflected off an object, the light changes direction, but it still travels in a straight line. For example, you can see moonlight reflected off water. This is light that has been reflected twice. First, sunlight was reflected off the Moon. Then it was reflected off the water to your eyes. If objects didn't reflect light, we wouldn't be able to see them.

How We See

We need reflected light to see. Our eyes are designed to see light. To see by reflected light, three things must happen:

- there must be a source of light
- the light must strike an object
- the light must be reflected from the object to your eye

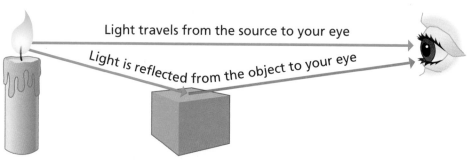

Light travels from the source to your eye

Light is reflected from the object to your eye

▲ We see things that reflect light to our eyes.

Reflections are very important. Almost every object we see, we see because light reflects off it. If you were in a room with no light, no reflections could reach your eyes and you would not be able to see. Bicycles, cars, some clothing, roads, and signs have reflectors that help us see them more easily when we shine a light on them.

▲ Reflected light keeps you safer at night.

Observe a Reflected Sunbeam

Skills Focus: observing, inferring, communicating

1. Use a small mirror to reflect a sunbeam onto a bicycle reflector that is at least 20 m away from you. How can you tell when you have hit the reflector with your reflected sunbeam?

Can you see all of your classmates' reflected sunbeams from where you are standing? Why do you think reflectors are designed to reflect light back to where it came from?

2. Use a magnifying glass to look at your reflector. What do you see?

 Do not try to reflect the sunlight into anybody's eyes or into windows.

⇨ Check Your Understanding

1. What three things must happen to be able to see something?
2. Is all the light you see reflected light? Explain your answer.
3. Why do some running shoes and jackets have reflective strips? When does this reflection work best? Why?

⇨ Learning Tip

To locate information for question 1, scan the section for text presented as three points.

4 Refraction

Predict Where to Aim a Spear

Skills Focus: observing, predicting, inferring, creating models

1. Put some water in a clear glass or clear plastic container. Place your pencil in the container of water so that it is leaning toward you and is touching the bottom on the far side of the container.

2. Look along the pencil from the top and observe if the pencil seems bent, straight, or in two pieces. Have your partner look from the side of the glass. Compare your observations. Where is the real tip of the pencil compared to the tip you see when looking along the pencil from the side?

3. Switch positions with your partner. Does this make a difference in your observations?

4. For many Aboriginal fishers in British Columbia, spearing salmon as they travel up the rivers to spawn is an important skill.

   • Predict where a person standing above the river should aim a spear when trying to spear a salmon: Right where the salmon appears to be? Above the salmon? Below the salmon? (Think of your experience with the pencil in the glass of water. Was the pencil point above or below where it appeared to be?)

   • Share your prediction with your classmates. Do they agree? Be prepared to explain your prediction.

▲ Spearing fish at Moricetown Canyon

Have you ever run from the beach into water? When you run into water, your body slows down. Light also moves more slowly through water. Light slows down when it passes from air into a solid or liquid that is transparent or translucent. If light enters the solid or liquid straight on, it goes right through. If light enters the solid or liquid at an angle and not straight, it not only slows down, it **refracts.** When light refracts, it bends. Now the light travels in a different direction. However, it will still travel in a straight line within the solid or liquid.

⮕ **Learning Tip**

Ask questions as you read. Ask yourself, "Why is refraction important? When does it happen? When doesn't it happen?"

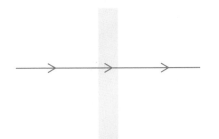

Air   Glass   Air
▲ Light that enters straight on goes right through.

Air   Glass   Air
▲ Light that enters at an angle refracts.

⮕ Check Your Understanding

1. Name three materials that would cause light to refract.

2. When is light passing through glass or water not refracted?

3. Birds such as kingfishers and ospreys have to look for fish and dive down to catch them. Think about what you learned about refraction of light in water. Do you think they dive directly down or at an angle? Explain your answer using a diagram.

Light Can Be Separated into Colours

Take Light Apart with a Bubble

Skills Focus: observing, inferring, communicating

1. Go outside and dip a wand in bubble solution and blow some bubbles. With a partner, look at one large bubble carefully. Can you see any colours on the bubble?

2. Write down the colours that you see. Where do you think the colours came from?

⇨ **Learning Tip**

Read more slowly if you find the ideas difficult to understand.

A **spectrum** is a band of colours that occurs when light is refracted and split. Sunlight is made of colours of light that mix together to make white light. The different colours in a spectrum are produced because each colour of light is refracted a different amount. In the Try This activity, you saw a band of colours, like a rainbow, on your bubble. You've seen rainbows in the sky or maybe in the spray of a sprinkler. Rainbows are created as sunlight is refracted and reflected by drops of water.

Observe What Colours Make Up White Light

Skills Focus: observing, inferring, communicating

1. Make a small hole (about 1 cm) in a piece of aluminum foil. Cover the end of a flashlight with the foil, making sure that the hole is near the centre of the light. Hold the foil on the flashlight with a rubber band.

2. Put a CD with the label face down on your desk. Ask your teacher to darken the classroom. Shine the flashlight on the CD. Experiment with the angle of the light to get the best spectrum.

3. Record the colours you see in the order they occur, starting with red. Do your classmates have the same colours in the same order? Are these the same colours you saw in the bubble activity?

Light can be split into colours if it passes through objects such as a crystal glass or a plastic suncatcher. A transparent piece of glass or plastic that can split light into a spectrum is called a **prism.**

When natural or artificial light is split into a spectrum, the order of colours in the spectrum is the same. You can use a memory helper called a mnemonic [nih-MAHN-ik] that sounds like a boy's name to remember the colours of a spectrum—ROY G BIV (**R**ed, **O**range, **Y**ellow, **G**reen, **B**lue, **I**ndigo, and **V**iolet). Today, scientists consider indigo and violet one colour. This changes the mnemonic to ROY G B'V. White light is a mixture of these colours.

Beam of white light entering prism

Prism

▲ How a triangular prism splits a beam of white light into a spectrum

➪ Check Your Understanding

1. How do you know that sunlight is made of different colours?

2. How can you break up sunlight into a spectrum?

3. Draw and colour a rainbow, putting the colours in the right order and labelling them.

Chapter Review

We can observe the properties of light.

Key Idea: Light travels in a straight line.

Vocabulary
light beam p. 97
light ray p. 97

Key Idea: Materials can be classified as transparent, translucent, or opaque.

Vocabulary
transparent p. 100
translucent p. 100
opaque p. 100

Key Idea: Materials can transmit, reflect, or absorb light.

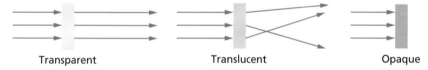

Transparent   Translucent   Opaque

Vocabulary
transmit p. 100
reflect p. 102
absorb p. 102

Key Idea: Our eyes can see light.

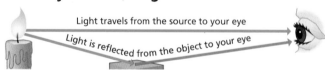

Light travels from the source to your eye

Light is reflected from the object to your eye

Key Idea: Light can be refracted.

Vocabulary
refract   p. 107

Key Idea: Light can be separated into colours.

Beam of white light entering prism

Prism

Vocabulary

spectrum p. 108
prism p. 109

Review Key Ideas and Vocabulary

Use the vocabulary words in your answers to the questions.

1. How can you tell that light travels in straight lines? Use a diagram in your answer.

2. What is a shadow and how is it formed?

3. Draw a table like the one below in your notebook. Use pictures or words to list four transparent materials, four translucent materials, and four opaque materials.

Transparent	Translucent	Opaque

4. Draw diagrams to show what happens when light strikes a piece of glass, a mirror, and a piece of black rock.

5. Why are you able to see things that do not produce light?

6. Describe how you would show someone that light can be refracted. Use a diagram in your answer.

7. What are the colours in the spectrum? (Remember to use your mnemonic with this question!)

Apply What You've Learned

Design and Build a Light Track

Looking Back

You have learned
- that light travels in straight lines
- that light can be reflected
- that light may be refracted when it passes from one material to another
- that light can be split into the colours of the rainbow

In this activity, you will design and build a light track that will show what you have learned about light.

Demonstrate Your Learning

Design and Build Your Light Track

1. Work with a partner or small group to design and build a light track in a shoebox (keep the lid of the shoebox for later). Cut a 3 cm hole in each end of the shoebox.

Put a flashlight at the beginning of the track and have a translucent screen at the end. The screen is the target for your light to hit. The light beam from the flashlight should not hit the screen directly. You may need to put in something to block the light. You will need to help your beam of light go around corners to reach the screen.

2. Your track should include as many of the following objects as possible. Some objects may belong to more than one of the categories below:
   - something transparent
   - something translucent
   - something opaque
   - something that will transmit light very well
   - something that will reflect light very well
   - something that will absorb light very well
   - something that will refract light
   - something that will split light into a spectrum
   - something that will colour the light

3. Arrange the design pieces you have chosen between the flashlight and the screen. Work in a darkened room.

4. When you have finished your light track, draw a diagram of it and label each of the objects you used. Use arrows to show the path of the light beam. Glue your diagram on top of the lid.

⇨ **Assessment Checklist**

LIGHT TRACK

As you make your light track, make sure that you show you are able to

✔ work cooperatively with other students
✔ identify materials that are transparent, translucent, and opaque
✔ identify materials that transmit, reflect, and absorb light well
✔ identify ways to split light into a spectrum
✔ use the properties of light to solve the problem
✔ use appropriate scientific words

Chapter 6

Sound is caused by vibrating objects.

→ **Key Ideas**

- Sound is a form of energy.
- Sound is caused by vibrations.
- Our ears can detect sound vibrations.

Each of the instruments in this picture makes a different sound. How do you think these instruments make sound?

We hear many sounds each day. Some sounds, like alarms, tell us things. Some, like music, we enjoy. Others we would rather not hear—like fingernails on a chalkboard. We also make sounds every day. But what is sound? What causes things, such as these instruments, to make sounds?

In this chapter, you will learn about the sources of sound.

What Is Sound?

Observe Sounds around You

Skills Focus: observing, communicating

1. Take your notebook and a pencil and find a place in the hallway of your school or on the playground where you can listen to sounds. Close your eyes and listen carefully. Make a list of all of the sounds that you hear.

2. After making your list, return to your classroom and observe how many sounds you can hear there. Sit as quietly as you can. Close your eyes to help you listen carefully. Make a list of what you hear.

3. Compare both of your lists with your classmates' lists.

You hear many sounds every day. But what is sound? Anything that can be heard—from a whisper, to cars on the street, to an airplane taking off—is called **sound.** There are some sounds humans cannot hear but other animals can hear. There are some sounds that no living things can hear. Noise is unwanted sound.

You learned that light is a form of **energy.** You also learned that energy is the ability to do work. Sound is another form of energy—it is energy that can be heard.

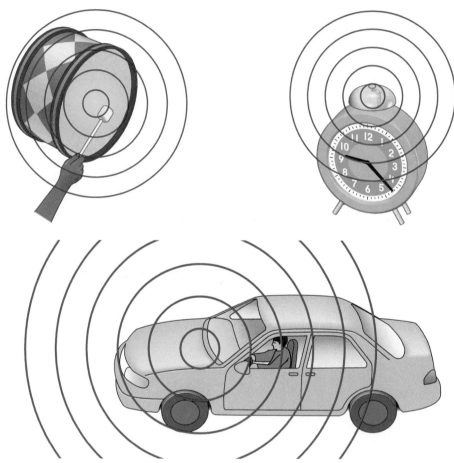

▲ What work are the sound makers above doing?

⇨ Check Your Understanding

1. How are sound and light the same?

Sound Is Caused by Vibrations

▲ What causes these sounds?

All sounds are caused by objects that are moving back and forth. We call a quick back-and-forth motion a **vibration** [vie-BRAY-shun]. Anything that makes sound is vibrating.

▲ What vibrates on a guitar to produce sound?

Did you know that when you make a sound a part of you is vibrating? When you talk or sing, two bands of tissue in your throat vibrate. These bands are called **vocal cords.** As you talk, sing, or shout, you push air from your lungs over your vocal cords to make them vibrate. This produces sound. Musical instruments also make sound using vibrations. For example, guitar strings vibrate to make sound.

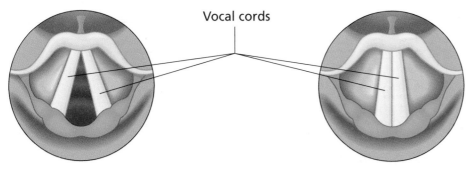

Vocal cords

Vocal cords open   Vocal cords closed

▲ When a person talks, the vocal cords close. Air from the lungs is forced between them, making them vibrate and produce sound.

Feel Sound Vibrations at Work

Skills Focus: observing, inferring, communicating

As you do each of the following activities, identify what is vibrating to produce the sound.

1. Place the fingers of one hand on the side of your throat and sing "eeeeee!" What do you feel? Sing the other vowel sounds. Try short vowels and long vowels. Do they all produce the same feeling in your fingers?

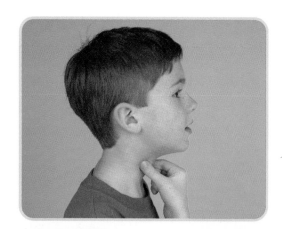

2. Use the palms of your hands to hold the ends of an inflated balloon. Move the side of the balloon close to, but not touching, your lips. Sing some vowel sounds, as you did in step 1. What do you feel?

3. Make a paper squawker. Fold a 15 cm strip of paper, 4 cm wide, in half. Fold each end outward about 2 cm to make a T-shape. With your hand held palm up, slide the T between your index and middle fingers so it is centred on the first finger joints. Make sure the flaps stay open, as they will be placed against your lips. Bring the open flaps of the T up to your lips with your fingers pointing toward the ceiling. Blow into the T so air passes through the slit, and adjust your finger pressure until you hear a sound. What is vibrating to make the sound?

In the last Try This activity, you felt sound vibrations. In the next activity, you will be able to see the result of sound vibrations.

118

See Sound Vibrations at Work

Skills Focus: observing, creating models

1. Your teacher will give you a can with both ends taken off. Cover one end of the can with plastic wrap. Hold the plastic on tightly with a rubber band. Now, place a pinch of sugar in the can.

2. Your teacher will have a portable stereo turned on its back, so that the speakers face the ceiling. The bass dial on the stereo should be turned up to maximum. Place the can so the plastic wrap is over the speaker of the stereo.

3. Turn up the volume of the music. What happens to the sugar? What is causing the sugar to "dance"? Can you see sound energy at work?

Like light, sound is a form of energy and can do work. Dentists and jewellers can even use sound with extremely fast vibrations for cleaning dental instruments and jewellery.

Did you know?

Sound made by extremely fast vibrations is called ultrasound. Humans cannot hear ultrasound. Doctors use ultrasound to quickly and safely see inside people's bodies. They can even see unborn babies.

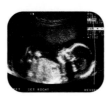

⇨ Check Your Understanding

1. What causes sound?

2. In the first Try This activity, you felt your throat as you sang, talked at a balloon, and made a paper squawker. Which one of these activities acted as a model of the vocal cords?

③ Detecting Sound Vibrations

You know that sounds exist because you hear them every day. But how do you hear them? You can hear because your ears can detect sound vibrations.

⭢ **Learning Tip**

As you read, use your finger to trace the path of sound vibrations on the diagram of the human ear.

The outside part of your ear catches sound vibrations and directs them to the ear canal. The vibrations travel down the ear canal to the eardrum and make it vibrate. The eardrum vibrations move little bones in the middle ear. The vibration of the little bones moves liquid inside the inner ear. The liquid then moves tiny hairs inside the ear. When these hairs are moved they send a message to the brain and we hear the sound.

The Human Ear

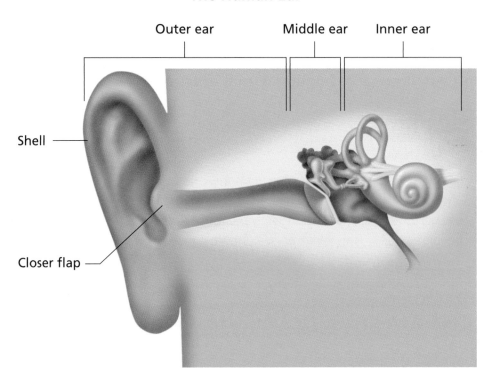

Change Your Hearing

Skills Focus: observing, inferring, communicating

1. Copy the following table in your notebook.

Change to ears	Sound from front of room	Sound from back of room
Normal ears		
Closed ear canals		
Outer ears (shells) forward		
Hands cupped backward		

2. Listen carefully as your teacher claps once from the front of the room. On a scale of 0 (you hear nothing) to 10 (you hear a loud sound), rate the sound and record the rating in your table.

3. Press your pointer fingers on the "closer flaps" to close your ear canals. Listen carefully while your teacher claps again. Rate this sound and record the rating in your table.

 Do not stick your fingers or other objects in your ears.

4. Cup your hands behind the shells of your ears and move the shells forward. Listen carefully while your teacher claps again. Rate the sound and add it to your table.

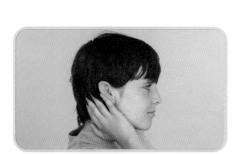

5. Cup your hands in front of your ears with your palms facing backward. Listen carefully while your teacher claps again. Rate the sound and add it to your table.

6. Your teacher will now move behind you. Repeat steps 2 to 5 with your teacher at the back of the classroom.

7. Share your ratings with your classmates. Discuss how moving your hands changed your hearing. Name some animals that can move their ears to hear sound better.

How Other Animals Detect Sound

Like humans, most animals have ears that allow them to detect vibrations and hear sound.

▲ We can see some ears easily, like those on a dog. Where do you think the ears are on an owl or seal?

Learning Tip

Read like a writer. Ask yourself, "Why did the authors choose these examples? Why did they include the photos? What can I learn, as a writer, from looking at this section?"

Other animals have body parts for hearing that are so different from our ears that we do not recognize them as ears. Sometimes these "ears" are in unexpected places.

▲ A cricket has "eardrums" on its front legs.

▲ A grasshopper has "eardrums" on its abdomen near where its back legs are attached.

Animals sense sound vibrations with many different parts of their bodies. Spiders sense vibrations with hairs on their legs, snakes feel vibrations in their lower jaw, and fish feel vibrations with a fluid-filled line along their sides.

▲ Snakes feel vibrations in their lower jaw. Fish feel vibrations with a fluid-filled line along their sides.

Animals use sound to communicate. Different sounds also warn them of danger and help them to find food.

Check Your Understanding

1. What does your ear detect that allows you to hear?
2. Why is it important not to put things in your ears?

Chapter Review

Sound is caused by vibrating objects.

Key Idea: Sound is a form of energy.

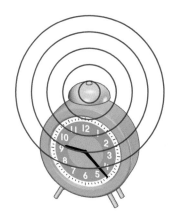

Vocabulary
sound p. 116
energy p. 116

Key Idea: Sound is caused by vibrations.

Vocal cords

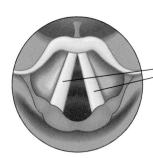

Vocal cords open

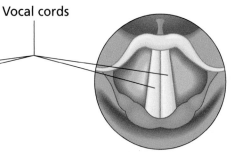

Vocal cords closed

Vocabulary
vibrations p. 117
vocal cords p. 117

Key Idea: Our ears can detect sound vibrations.

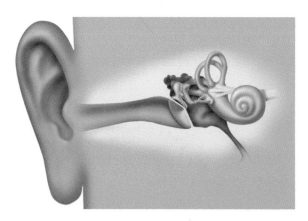

Review Key Ideas and Vocabulary

Use the vocabulary words in your answers to the questions.

1. What is sound?

2. What causes sound?

3. How is sound being made in each of the following photographs?

4. What part of your body detects sound vibrations best?

Make a Sound Map of Your School

Looking Back

You have learned

- that sound is a form of energy you can hear
- that your ears can detect sound vibrations from many sources

In this activity, you will use what you have learned to observe and record the sounds around your school. You will use the information you collect to make a sound map of your school and schoolyard.

Demonstrate Your Learning

Make a Sound Map

1. Your teacher will show you a map of your school and schoolyard and will assign you and your partner one part of the school or schoolyard to sit in and listen for sounds.

2. Once in your assigned area, listen and observe carefully. Do not rush. Be careful not to miss soft sounds. Write down all the sounds you hear and what you think has made them. Once you have finished listening, you and your partner should combine your lists into one list.

3. Return to the classroom and post your list beside the map. Place a string between your listening spot and your list.

4. Now, take a look at the sound map your class created. As a class, decide which listening spot would be
   - the quietest to read in
   - the hardest to hear a secret in
   - filled with the greatest variety of sounds
   - best to sit in and listen to birds

⇨ Assessment Checklist

SOUND MAP

As you are creating your sound map, make sure to show you are able to

- ✔ work cooperatively with other students
- ✔ identify sources of sound
- ✔ communicate clearly

We can observe the properties of sound.

- Sound travels in waves.

- Large vibrations cause loud sound; small vibrations cause soft sound.

- High frequency causes high sound; low frequency causes low sound.

- Sound can travel through gases, liquids, or solids.

- Materials can transmit, reflect, or absorb sound.

You hear many sounds every day. Some sounds are loud, like an airplane taking off, and some are very soft, like a whisper. Some sounds are very low and deep, like music from a tuba, and some are high and squeaky, like the squeak of a mouse. Some sounds are nice to listen to, such as music. Others are noisy and unpleasant, like screeching tires. Why are there so many kinds of sounds? Why aren't all sounds the same?

In this chapter, you will learn about some of the properties of sound. You will learn how these properties make sound different.

Sound Waves

Try This

Observe Waves

Skills Focus: observing, inferring

1. With a partner, stretch a Slinky about 2–3 m. Sit down and rest the stretched Slinky on the floor, but do not let the Slinky go.

2. Get your partner to start a wave at one end by pinching together several coils and then releasing the pinched coils all at once. What do you see? Take turns making waves.

Sound travels like the waves you created in the Slinky. Sound is caused by vibrations. We call each vibration a **sound wave.** As an object vibrates it produces sound waves. Sound waves must travel through a material to be heard.

Check Your Understanding

1. What is a sound wave?

② Loudness

▲ Which makes a louder sound?

Sound can be loud or soft. The **loudness** of a sound depends on the size of the vibrations of a sound wave. The loudness of a sound is called its **volume.** What makes some sound louder than other sound? How can you change the volume of a sound?

Make Sounds Loud, Louder, and Loudest!

Skills Focus: observing, inferring, communicating

Try these activities. Be sure to write notes about each activity.

1. Place a 30 cm ruler on your desk so that about 12 cm hangs over the edge. With one hand, firmly hold the ruler about 2 cm back from the edge of your desk. Now, gently strum the other end of the ruler to make sound waves. What do you hear? Strum a little more softly and see what happens to the volume of the sound. Strum harder, but not so hard that you break the ruler! What happened to the volume of the sound?

2. Stretch a rubber band around a small, sturdy box. Very gently stretch the rubber band about 1 cm and let it go. Look at the band vibrating and listen to the sound. Stretch the band a bit farther and listen as you look. Stretch the band even farther and listen to the sound again. What happens to the sound?

3. Now, look at your notes and, in your notebook, write a statement about what size of vibration makes a loud sound and what size makes a soft sound.

As you saw in the Try This activity, the louder the sound is, the larger the vibrations are. An object with large vibrations has a large amount of energy and creates a loud sound. An object with small vibrations has a small amount of energy and creates a soft sound.

Check Your Understanding

1. What happens to a sound when vibrations get bigger?

2. What would a musician do to get each of these instruments to make a louder sound?

3 Pitch

▲ Can you sing in both a low voice and a high voice?

Can you sing a scale, like do re mi? When you sing a scale, you start on a low note and then sing high notes. **Pitch** is how high or low a sound is. How can you change the pitch of a sound?

Observe Pitch

Skills Focus: observing, inferring, communicating

Try these two activities. Be sure to write notes about each activity.

1. **Singing comb.** Use a comb to make a sound. Run an index card over the teeth of a comb to make a sound. What do you have to do to make a sound with a lower pitch? What do you have to do to make a sound with a higher pitch?

2. **Spinning penny.** Find a Canadian penny that has a date from 1982 to 1996. These pennies have 12 sides.

3. Stretch the mouth of a balloon open and push the penny inside. Blow up the balloon so that it's almost full. Tie the balloon closed. Hold the balloon at chest height with the tied end of the balloon in one palm and the round end of the balloon in the other.

4. Quickly move your hands together in a circle away from you as shown in the picture on the right. Do not shake the balloon. You are doing it correctly when you stop moving the balloon and the penny keeps spinning. Let the penny continue to spin by itself, and listen to the sound. Does the pitch get higher or lower as the penny slows down and there are fewer vibrations per second?

5. Look at your notes and, in your notebook, write a statement that explains how the number of vibrations per second changes the pitch of a sound.

As you saw in the Try This activity, more vibrations per second produce a higher pitch and fewer vibrations per second produce a lower pitch. The number of vibrations per second is called **frequency** [FREE-kwun-see]. The frequency makes the pitch of a sound high or low.

⇨ Check Your Understanding

1. What happens to a sound when the number of vibrations per second is increased?

2. What do you think is happening to the frequency of your vocal cords as you sing up a scale (do re mi)?

4 What Sounds Do Animals Hear?

▲ This dog is responding to a special whistle that dogs can hear but people cannot hear.

Have you ever seen someone use a dog whistle? The pitch of a dog whistle is very high. The sound is so high pitched that people cannot hear it. Only dogs can hear the sound.

Sometimes animals make noises and we do not even notice. The Richardson's ground squirrel, sometimes called a gopher, can call warnings to other squirrels. Humans cannot hear the ground squirrel's call because it is above the range of human hearing.

Scientists used to think that giraffes did not make any sound at all. They now know that giraffes do make sound. The sound is just too low pitched for humans to hear.

▲ This Richardson's ground squirrel is ready to sound a high-pitched warning call. Other ground squirrels will hear its call but humans will not.

▲ Humans cannot hear giraffe voices because they are too low pitched.

Scientists call one vibration per second one Hertz (Hz). Young humans with good hearing can hear sound when the vibrations range from about 20 Hz to 20 000 Hz. Since humans cannot hear giraffes, the sound produced by giraffes must be lower than 20 Hz.

This bar graph compares the range of hearing for humans and other animals.

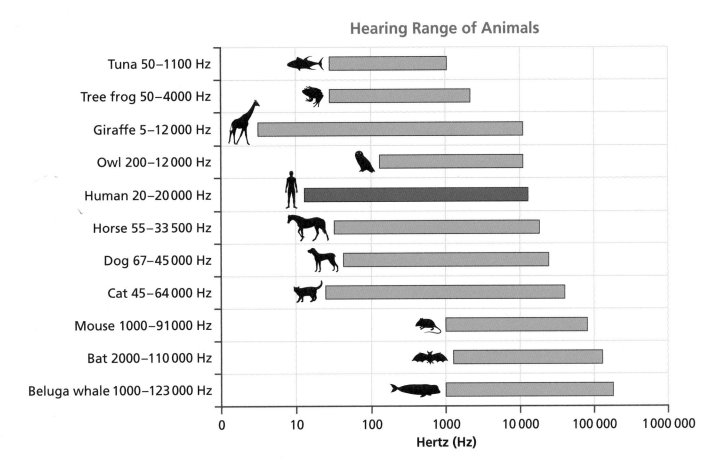

Hearing Range of Animals

Check Your Understanding

1. What animal(s) can hear sounds that are too low in pitch for you to hear?

2. List some animals that can hear sounds that are too high in pitch for you to hear?

3. Are there any two animals that cannot hear any of the same sounds? If so, which ones?

5 *Conduct an Investigation*

○ SKILLS MENU

○ Questioning   ○ Classifying

● Predicting   ● Inferring

● Observing   ● Interpreting Data

○ Measuring   ● Communicating

What Materials Can Sound Travel Through?

You learned that light can travel through some materials but not others. What materials do you think sound can travel through?

In this investigation, you will work with a partner and will discover what materials sound can travel through.

Question

Can sound travel through gases, liquids, or solids?

Prediction

Copy the following table in your notebook. Predict whether sound can travel through a gas, liquid, or solid. Write your predictions in the first column of your table.

Data Table for Investigation 7.5	Prediction	Result
Can sound travel through gases (air)?		
Can sound travel through liquids (water)?		
Can sound travel through solids (wood or metal tabletop)?		

metal spoons

tub of water

Materials

- 2 metal spoons
- plastic tub full of water

Step 1 Stand 1 m from your partner. Talk quietly. Can you hear each other? Can sound travel through air (a gas)? Record your result in your table.

Step 2 Click two metal spoons together 20 cm from your partner's ear. Now, get your partner to put one ear against a plastic tub full of water. Click the spoons together under the water, making sure you do not touch the plastic tub. Can your partner hear them? Can sound travel through water (a liquid)? Record your result in your table.

Step 3 Stand at one end of a table and get your partner to stand at the other end facing away from you. Practise scratching the table with your fingernail so lightly that your partner cannot hear it when listening 5 cm above the table. Then get your partner to put one ear right against the end of the table while still facing away. Scratch the table again. Can your partner hear it? Can sound travel through a solid? Record your result in your table.

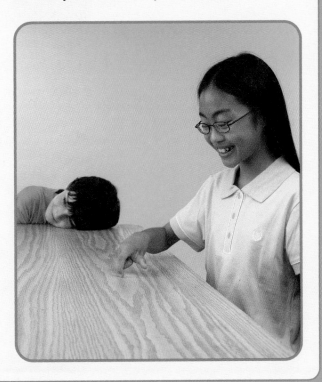

Interpret Data and Observations

1. Look at your table. Can sound travel through gases? Can sound travel through liquids? Can sound travel through solids? Write a sentence that describes the types of materials that sound can travel through.

2. Which of your predictions were correct?

Apply and Extend

1. There is no air in space. Do you think it is possible to hear in space? Why or why not?

2. Look at the photo below. Do you think that a swimmer under water would be able to hear the boat? Why or why not?

⇨ Check Your Understanding

1. Why did you need to work with a partner in these activities?

2. What is the advantage of thinking about the question and making predictions before you conduct an investigation?

Transmitting Sounds 6

In the last section, you learned that sound can travel through gases, liquids, and solids. These materials **transmit** sound when they allow sound to pass through them. Most of the sound vibrations that we hear come to our ears through the air, a gas. But we can also hear through liquids and solids.

Sound travels faster through liquids than through gases. It travels even faster through solids.

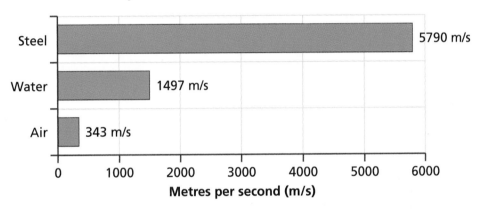

The Speed of Sound in Different Materials

Steel — 5790 m/s
Water — 1497 m/s
Air — 343 m/s
Metres per second (m/s)

Did you know?

Sound travels through warm air at about 343 m/s (metres per second). That is close to 1 km (1000 m) in 3 seconds. Light travels nearly a million times faster—at about 300 000 000 m/s. If a light and a sound are produced at the same time, we will see the light before we hear the sound. For example, we see a bolt of lightning before we hear the thunder.

Think back to how the ear works. For us to be able to hear sound, vibrations have to travel through a gas (air) to the ear. The vibrations then travel through two solids, the eardrum and the little bones in the ear. Finally, the vibrations move through the liquid in your inner ear.

⇨ Check Your Understanding

1. What types of materials can sound travel through?
2. What does sound usually travel through to reach your ears?
3. Does the sound of clicking spoons travel faster through air or through water?

7 Reflecting Sounds

▲ Your voice sounds very different if you speak into a container.

Have you ever been in an empty space that sounded hollow? Have you ever spoken into a pail or a stairwell and been amazed at how different your voice sounded? Perhaps you have been in a thunderstorm when the sound of the thunder seemed to last for several seconds as the sound reflected off rocky hillsides. All those experiences were the result of sound reflecting off surfaces.

Not all of the sound vibrations that reach some materials pass through them. Some materials can **reflect** some of the sound vibrations.

Model the Reflection of a Sound Wave

Skills Focus: observing, inferring

Form a group with two other students.

1. Take a Slinky and stretch it out about 2–3 m between two of you. Sit down and rest the stretched Slinky on the floor. Have the third person act as an observer.

2. Have one partner hold the end of the Slinky firmly so it will not move. The other partner starts a wave at one end by pinching together five coils and then letting them go all at once. Get the observer to watch for the wave to bounce back. Put a piece of tape on the floor to mark how far the wave was reflected.

3. Repeat step 2, but this time pinch ten coils and let them go. Does this model of a louder sound (more coils used) produce a louder echo?

Hard, smooth surfaces reflect the most sound vibrations. Sometimes we can hear the reflection. We call a sound wave that is reflected back from a hard surface an **echo** [EK-oh].

You can make an echo by bouncing the sound of your voice off a hard surface like a wall or a cliff. If you are too close to the reflecting surface, you will not hear the echo. You have to be at least 17 m away from the wall or cliff to hear an echo. The echo will take longer to get back to you if you are farther away from the hard surface.

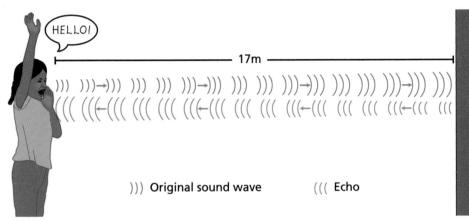

))) Original sound wave   (((Echo

▲ This is how you make an echo.

⇨ Check Your Understanding

1. What type of surface reflects sound vibrations?
2. Describe how you could make an echo.
3. What would you have to do to make an echo take longer to come back to you?

8 Absorbing Sounds

Sometimes we do not want to hear loud sounds or echoes. How can we keep things quiet when sound waves travel so easily through air and reflect off surfaces?

Compare Rooms

Skills Focus: observing, measuring, interpreting data, inferring

1. Go into the middle of the school gymnasium and clap. Listen to the sound until it fades away. Silently count how many seconds it takes for the sound to fade by thinking, "One elephant, two elephant, ..."
2. Now, try the same thing inside your classroom.
3. How long did it take for the sound to fade away in the gymnasium? How long did it take for the sound to fade away in the classroom? What might have caused any difference?

Materials with soft surfaces do not transmit or reflect sound well. The sound vibrations get trapped, and echo back and forth, in little air pockets in these materials. We can say that these materials **absorb** sound. Your home may have carpets, drapes, and soft furniture that absorb sound.

◀ Living rooms are filled with soft surfaces that absorb sound.

142

We use soft materials to absorb sound vibrations so that there are fewer sound vibrations reflected. Theatres have soft seats and curtains so they do not have echoes like gymnasiums.

◀ The Queen Elizabeth Theatre in Vancouver has a ceiling that prevents echoes.

We also use soft materials to absorb some sound vibrations so that sounds are not too loud. A car is lined with soft materials like foam and fabric so that the sounds of the engine and the wheels on the road are absorbed.

▲ Soft fabrics absorb sounds in a car interior.

⇨ **Learning Tip**

Determine what is most important by looking at the photos. What do the photos of the living room, the theatre, and the car interior have in common?

⇨ Check Your Understanding

1. What type of surface absorbs sound vibrations?
2. Give three examples of where we use materials that absorb sound. For each example, explain why we want to absorb some or all of the sound.

Chapter Review

We can observe the properties of sound.

Key Idea: Sound travels in waves.

Vocabulary
sound wave
p. 129

Key Idea: Large vibrations cause loud sound; small vibrations cause soft sound.

Vocabulary
loudness p. 130
volume p. 130

Key Idea: High frequency causes high sound; low frequency causes low sound.

Vocabulary
pitch p. 132
frequency p. 133

Key Idea: Sound can travel through gases, liquids, or solids.

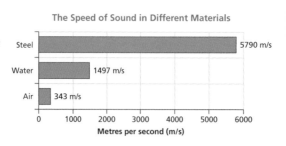

The Speed of Sound in Different Materials

Steel — 5790 m/s
Water — 1497 m/s
Air — 343 m/s

0   1000   2000   3000   4000   5000   6000
Metres per second (m/s)

Key Idea: Materials can transmit, reflect, or absorb sound.

Vocabulary

transmit p. 139
reflect p. 140
echo p. 141
absorb p. 142

Transmit

Absorb

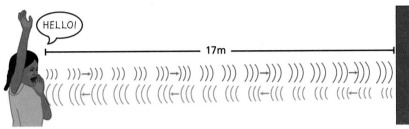

Reflect

Review Key Ideas and Vocabulary

Use the vocabulary words in your answers to the questions.

1. How does sound travel?

2. If you make vibrations bigger, what happens to the loudness of the sound? If you make vibrations smaller, what happens to the loudness of the sound?

3. If you make an object vibrate at a higher frequency, what happens to the pitch of the sound it makes? If an object vibrates at a lower frequency, what happens to the pitch of the sound it makes?

4. Give two examples of sounds that humans cannot hear. Why can't humans hear these sounds?

5. Can sound travel through water? Can it travel through solid objects such as walls?

6. Give an example of a reflected sound.

7. What types of materials absorb sound well? When might you want to have sound absorbed?

Apply What You've Learned

Build a Sound Maker

Looking Back

You have learned
- about many properties of sound
- how to make sounds louder and higher pitched
- what materials transmit sound well
- that sound can also be reflected and absorbed

In this activity, you will use what you have learned to build a sound maker.

Demonstrate Your Learning

Build a Sound Maker

1. Work individually or with a partner to plan a sound maker that can make loud or soft sounds and has more than one pitch. What will vibrate to produce the sounds? How can you make the sounds louder or softer? How will you change the pitch?

2. Draw a design for your sound maker. Show your design to your teacher. Once you have your teacher's approval, build your sound maker.

3. Now, play your sound maker. Do you like the sound? Can you change the loudness of your sound maker? Can you change the pitch? If it does not work very well, you can change the design, or make another sound maker using different materials.

4. Make up a name for your sound maker. Demonstrate it to the class. Explain how it works.

⇨ Assessment Checklist

SOUND MAKER

As you build your sound maker, make sure to show you are able to

✔ identify what is vibrating to make the sound
✔ change the loudness of the sound it makes
✔ change the pitch of the sound it makes
✔ use appropriate scientific words when explaining your sound maker

Making Connections

Put On a Play!

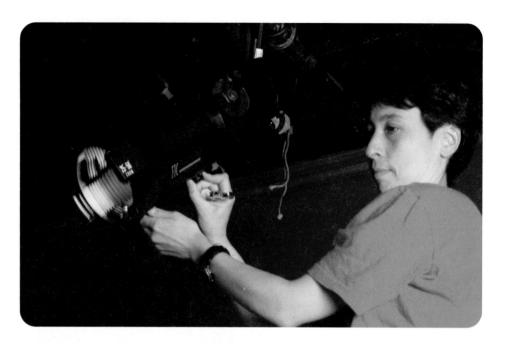

Looking Back

In this unit, you have learned
- about many sources of light and sound
- about the properties of light and sound

In this activity, you will use what you have learned to do the light and sound effects for a play. When people put on a play, they use light and sound effects to make their play more interesting.

Lighting technicians use artificial light sources to light the stage. Sometimes the artificial light sources are supposed to look like natural light sources such as the Sun or the stars in the night sky. Lighting technicians need to understand the properties of light to use light effectively.

Sound technicians figure out how to make realistic sound effects. They might make a sound like thunder or like a police siren. Sound technicians need to understand the properties of sound to make their sounds realistic and exciting.

Demonstrate Your Learning

Developing Light and Sound Effects for a Play

1. You will work in a small group. You will need a story for your play. You can make up a new story or change a story you know to include as many of the following as possible:

   - the sound of rain
   - thunder
   - a rainbow
   - loud and soft sounds
   - animals that can hear sounds that people cannot hear

   - lightning
   - a starry sky
   - a shadow
   - high-pitched and low-pitched sounds
   - an echo
   - a reflection

2. Perform your play for the class. Be prepared to point out to your teacher where you have included each of the things on the list above.

⇨ Assessment Checklist

LIGHT EFFECTS

As you do the lighting for your play, make sure you show you are able to

✔ work cooperatively with other students
✔ use the properties of light to make effective light effects
✔ use appropriate scientific words to describe the sources and properties of light

SOUND EFFECTS

As you do the sound effects for your play, make sure you show you are able to

✔ work cooperatively with other students
✔ use the properties of sound to make effective sound effects
✔ use appropriate scientific words to describe the sources and properties of sound

Preview

What part of British Columbia do you call home? Is it flat or are there mountains? Is it wet or dry? How does your home area provide you with what you need to survive and be healthy?

Plants and animals also need home areas that provide the things they need to survive. There are many kinds of plants and animals. Some do better in one type of home area and some do better in another.

In this unit, you will learn about the different types of home areas of plants and animals. You will also learn how plants and animals are suited to their home areas. You will learn how plants and animals affect each other when they live in the same home area and what happens if their home area is changed in some way. Learning about plants and animals will give you a better understanding of the world around you.

Describe Home

Skills Focus: communicating

1. Draw a large circle in your notebook. Write the word "Home" at the top of the circle.

2. In the circle, use the questions at the beginning of the Preview to describe your home. Add more details about your home. (Is it warm or cold? Do you live in a house or apartment?) Compare your work with a classmate's work.

◀ These raccoons are using a dead or dying tree for their home.

Adaptations help organisms survive in their habitats.

- ▶ Different habitats have different features.

- ▶ Adaptations help organisms survive in different habitats.

- ▶ Adaptations can be structures.

- ▶ Adaptations can be behaviours or responses.

- ▶ Organisms live in habitats that have the conditions they need to grow and survive.

Sea otters spend almost their whole lives in the ocean. Why can a sea otter live so well in the ocean? The water is cold but the sea otter has very thick fur to keep it warm. It has webbed back feet for swimming. The sea otter dives deep in the water for food and can stay underwater for up to five minutes. Sometimes it puts a rock on its chest and uses it to break the shells of the sea urchins it eats. The sea otter sometimes ties itself in huge seaweed called kelp to keep from floating away while it sleeps at night.

A sea otter is well suited to its ocean home, but humans can't survive in the ocean. What makes an area good for one animal but not another? In this chapter, you will learn why plants and animals can live in some areas but not others.

What Habitats Provide

Living things are called **organisms.** Both plants and animals are living things. All organisms need a living space or home.

The home of an organism is called its **habitat.** Habitats are different sizes. Some are as large as a forest. Others are as small as a single tree. Organisms live in habitats that meet their needs.

Plants need four things to survive. These are
- sunlight
- water
- nutrients
- the appropriate temperature range

Plants can only grow and survive in habitats where these needs are met.

Like plants, animals need four things to survive. These are
- food
- water
- shelter
- the appropriate temperature range

Like plants, animals live in habitats that meet their needs. If an animal's needs are not met, then the animal will die or leave the area.

▲ This garden plant was missing something in its habitat, so it died.

⇨ Check Your Understanding

1. Draw a Venn diagram to compare the needs of plants and animals.

2. Think of a pet you have or that you know about. Write a sentence explaining how the pet meets each of its four needs.

2 Different Habitats Have Different Features

British Columbia has many different types of habitats. What makes one habitat different from another? It is the features each habitat has that make them different. There are five important features that each habitat shares.

Light

Some habitats in British Columbia have sunny weather. Other habitats are cloudy and do not get as much light from the Sun.

▲ Some habitats in British Columbia get more sunlight than other habitats.

Water

Some habitats are wetter than other habitats. British Columbia has ocean habitats, river habitats, and wet forest habitats. It also has drier habitats such as grasslands and deserts.

▲ The Khutzeymateen [K'TZIM-a-deen] Valley gets more precipitation than the interior grasslands. The antelope brush shown here is a type of plant found in the grasslands.

▷ Learning Tip

As you read, make connections to what you already know. Ask yourself, "How does this fit with what I know?"

Temperature

Different habitats have different temperature ranges. A temperature range is the difference between the highest and lowest temperature. Habitats that are farther north or higher up the mountains are colder. Some habitats, such as deserts, can be very hot during the day and very cold at night. All habitats in Canada are colder in winter than in summer.

▲ Even on a summer day, mountain habitats can be much colder than other habitats.

Learning Tip

As you read, make personal connections. Ask yourself, "How do I get food and water from my habitat?"

Food

Different habitats contain different kinds of food. All organisms need food to grow and survive.

▲ A deer lives in a habitat that provides the food it needs.

Shelter

Different habitats provide different types of shelter. Some types of shelter are plants, rocks, soil, or water. Some animals live in burrows in the ground. A burrow is a hole in the ground that an animal can live in. Birds build nests from materials found in their habitats.

▲ Many birds build nests in trees.

Compare Two Habitats

Skills Focus: observing, classifying, inferring, communicating

1. Copy the table below in your notebook. Use it to compare the two habitats in the photos.

		Pond habitat	Desert habitat
	Amount of sunlight		
	Amount of water		
	Temperature		
	Food		
	Shelter		

2. Are there any ways in which the habitats are similar?

Check Your Understanding

1. What is a habitat?
2. List five ways that habitats can be different from one another.
3. Describe the habitat near your home.

Learning Tip

To locate the answer to question 2, scan the headings in this section.

3 Conduct an Investigation

SKILLS MENU

○ Questioning   ○ Classifying
● Predicting   ● Inferring
● Observing   ● Interpreting Data
● Measuring   ● Communicating

What Is the Best Habitat for Mealworms?

A mealworm looks like a worm but it is really a larva that will grow into a beetle. Mealworms like to eat bran. They also eat decaying leaves, sticks, and grasses. Many animals, such as lizards, spiders, and birds, eat mealworms.

In this investigation, you will set up different habitats for mealworms to see which habitats they like better.

Question

What is the best habitat for mealworms?
  • Do mealworms prefer a dry or wet habitat?
  • Do mealworms prefer a light or dark habitat?

Prediction

Write a prediction that describes the kind of habitat the mealworms will prefer: dry or wet, and light or dark.

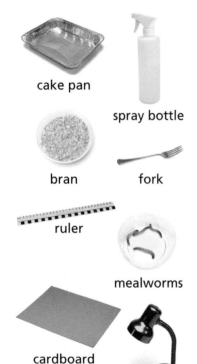

cake pan

spray bottle

bran   fork

ruler

mealworms

cardboard

lamp

Materials

  • 22 cm × 33 cm cake pan
  • bran
  • ruler
  • cardboard
  • spray bottle of water
  • fork
  • mealworms
  • gooseneck lamp

✋ Be sure not to harm the mealworms. Wash your hands well before and after handling the mealworms.

Your teacher will set up two stations. With your group, go to each station and follow the steps. You will repeat some of the steps at each station. Each time you try the steps, it is called a trial. If you do two trials, you do the steps twice. Once you have finished all of your trials at both stations, your teacher will collect your mealworms in a jar of bran.

In your notebook, make a table like the one below to record what you observe at each station.

Data Table for Investigation 8.3	Trial 1	Trial 2
Number of mealworms in the light part		
Number of mealworms in the dark part		
Number of mealworms in the dry part		
Number of mealworms in the wet part		

Wet and Dry Station

Step 1 Fill your cake pan with bran to a depth of 3 cm.

Step 2 Use a piece of cardboard to separate the two halves of the cake pan.

Step 3 Spray one half of the pan with water. Mix the bran lightly with a fork. Spray and mix until all of the bran is wet. Do not do anything to the other side of the pan.

Step 4 Carefully remove the cardboard. Place 10 mealworms at the centre of the pan.

Step 5 Observe the mealworms for 10 minutes. Write what you observe.

Step 6 Count the number of mealworms in each half of the pan after 10 minutes. Write this data in your table.

Step 7 Put the mealworms in the centre of the pan again and repeat steps 5 and 6.

Light and Dark Station

Step 1 Fill your cake pan with bran to a depth of 3 cm.

Step 2 Use the piece of cardboard to make a roof over one half of the pan.

Step 3 Place the lamp over the other half of the pan.

 Be careful not to touch the lamp while it is on as it will get very hot.

Step 4 Place 10 mealworms in the pan, along the edge of the cardboard.

Step 5 Observe the mealworms for 10 minutes. Write what you observe.

Step 6 Count the number of mealworms in each half of the pan after 10 minutes. Write this data in your table.

Step 7 Place the mealworms along the edge of the cardboard again and repeat steps 5 and 6.

⇨ Learning Tip

For more information on bar graphs, see the Skills Handbook, page 235.

Interpret Data and Observations

1. Create a bar graph using the data you collected at each station. Make a graph for each station.

2. Compare your observations and data with other groups. Were their observations and data the same or different? If they were different, can you explain why?

3. Using the information from all the groups, write a sentence about the type of habitat mealworms seem to prefer.

4. Were your predictions correct?

Apply and Extend

1. In this investigation, you learned whether mealworms preferred a wet or dry habitat and a light or dark habitat. What would you do to find out whether mealworms liked a warm habitat or a cool habitat?

2. Add plants, such as celery leaves, carrot tops, or pine cones, to one half of an empty cake pan. Place 10 mealworms at the centre of the pan. Observe the mealworms for 10 minutes. Write what you observe.

Check Your Understanding

1. Why was it important to watch your mealworms for a full 10 minutes at each station?

2. Why was it important to do two trials at each station?

3. What could you do if you got different results in your two trials?

4 What Are Adaptations?

If you look closely at plants and animals, you will observe they have features that make them well suited to the habitat that they live in.

The blue heron has long legs for wading in water. It has a pointed bill for fishing. It stays very still or moves slowly and smoothly, so it does not frighten fish. These features make the blue heron well suited for life in a marsh or river.

▶ Blue herons have long legs for wading and pointed bills for fishing.

The pond lily has a long stem that helps get its leaves close to the surface of the water. The leaves are large and float on the surface of the water where they can get sunlight. These features make the pond lily well suited to life in a pond.

▶ Lily pads are the leaves of pond lilies. They float on the surface of water so they can get more sunlight.

Humans also have features that help them meet needs in their habitats. Your thumb is a feature that makes many things easier for you.

Try This

Life Without a Thumb

Skills Focus: observing

1. Use a piece of masking tape to tape one thumb across the palm of your hand. Tape the thumb of the hand you use the most.

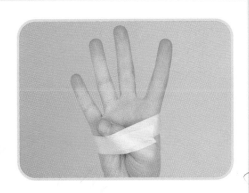

2. Try to do a few everyday activities: write your name, tie your shoes, or button your shirt. How did not having a thumb affect the way you did these activities? Can you think of other activities that you would have trouble doing without your thumb?

A way in which an organism is suited to its habitat is called an **adaptation** [AD-ap-TAY-shun]. Plants and animals have adaptations that make them well suited to their habitats. There are two main types of adaptations— structural [STRUK-chur-uhl] adaptations and behavioural [bih-HAYV-yur-uhl] adaptations.

Check Your Understanding

1. What is an adaptation?
2. Give two examples of an adaptation.

Learning Tip

To locate the information you need to answer these questions, scan the photos and key words in this section.

5 Structural Adaptations

Some adaptations are body parts. Body parts are also known as structures. These structures can help organisms live in their habitats.

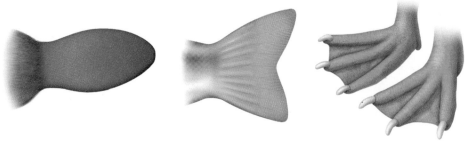

▲ In what kind of habitat would you find these structures?

When you see structures like these, you know the animal lives in a watery habitat. These structures help animals like beavers, fish, and ducks survive in their habitat. Both plants and animals have different structures depending on their habitat.

Structures That Help Plants Adapt

Some plants have adaptations that allow them to survive in shady places. The adaptations help them make the best use of the light.

Plants that live in the shade usually have large leaves. The larger the leaf, the more sunlight it can collect. A leaf can collect even more sunlight if it is spread out. That is why the pink wintergreen has wide, round leaves instead of thin, narrow ones. The leaves also lie flat to help them catch more light.

▲ The leaves of this pink wintergreen catch more light because they are spread out and lie flat.

Plants also have structures to help them adapt to dry habitats. The leaves of plants that live in dry habitats are small. Small leaves lose less water through evaporation than large leaves. The leaves of a cactus are so small you might not even realize they are leaves.

▲ What structure helps this cactus live in its dry habitat?

Structures That Help Animals Adapt

Many animals have teeth to help them get and chew food. Animals that eat meat have sharp, pointy teeth that are good for tearing meat. Animals that eat plants have flat teeth that are good for grinding up plants. Animals that eat both meat and plants have both kinds of teeth.

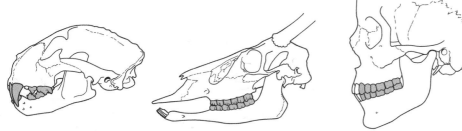

▲ Which teeth belong to a plant eater? Which teeth belong to a meat eater? Which teeth belong to an organism that eats both plants and meat?

Some animals use their tongues to get their food. Butterflies unroll their long tongues to get the nectar in flowers. Frogs have long sticky tongues to catch insects.

▲ Butterflies and frogs both use their tongues to get food.

▲ Danger for the snail can be a hungry duck or hot, dry weather.

Many animals have adaptations that allow them to hide in their habitats. A badger has powerful claws for digging a burrow. Some animals, like turtles and snails, have tough body parts to hide in when danger gets too close. Their hard outer shells are adaptations that help protect them. When they are attacked, they can pull soft body parts into their shells. When danger passes, they will come out again.

Some animals can hide in plain sight. They have body markings and colours that make them difficult to see in their habitats. We say they are camouflaged [CAM-uh-flazhd].

▲ Pacific tree frogs can change colour quickly to hide in their habitats.

Camouflage a Potato

Skills Focus: observing, inferring

1. Go for a walk in a natural area near your school. Observe the colours and shapes that you see.

2. Take a potato and try to camouflage it so that it will be hard to find in this habitat. You can use toothpicks to stick things on it that are found in the habitat, like leaves and twigs, but do not completely cover it. "Hide" your camouflaged potato in plain view. See if your classmates can find it.

Many animals have adaptations that allow them to be active and warm in the winter. The snowshoe hare and the caribou both have feet that widen. This helps in the snowy season, when the animals need to travel. A wider foot makes it easier for animals to stay on top of the snow. Caribou have two layers of fur covering their bodies. This keeps the heat in. They have many short hairs covering their nose and nostrils. This keeps the nose warm as they push it through the snow, searching for plants to eat.

⇨ Learning Tip

Check your understanding of this paragraph. Sketch a caribou and label its adaptations.

▲ Caribou can move more easily in snow because they have feet that widen.

⇨ Check Your Understanding

1. Name and describe one structure that helps plants adapt.
2. Draw and label pictures to show three different ways animals hide.
3. Name two structures that may help an animal in winter.

6 # Behavioural Adaptations

▲ A Great Basin spadefoot toad hunts in the night when it is cool.

Adaptations can also be behaviours. The way animals act in their habitats helps them survive.

Behaviours That Help Animals Adapt

Animals that live in dry habitats have adaptations for surviving on little water. Many desert animals look for shelter in the shade. Some desert animals are only active at night when it is cooler. These behaviours prevent them from losing water in the hot sun.

Some animals have behaviours that are adaptations for protection. Many animals that live in groups use warning signals to tell each other when danger is near. Musk oxen in Canada's far north form a circle when wolves attack them. The musk oxen put their young inside the circle to protect them. The adult musk oxen stand facing out, ready to attack the wolves with their horns.

▲ The hoary marmot is sometimes called a "whistler" because of the sound it makes to warn other marmots when danger is near.

▲ The horns facing out help protect adult musk oxen from attacking wolves. The young are inside the circle for safety.

Some animals migrate to another place in winter in order to find food and shelter. Some, like bighorn sheep, do not migrate far. Bighorn sheep spend summers high in the mountains. They move to the valleys in winter to find food.

▲ Bighorn sheep move from the mountains to valleys in winter.

Other animals migrate much farther. Many birds in British Columbia gather into flocks in the fall and fly south where the weather is warmer. In the winter, the rufous hummingbird needs to go where the weather is warm enough for its food to grow.

▲ The rufous hummingbird migrates to Mexico in the winter.

Some animals, such as chipmunks and groundhogs, hibernate for most of the winter. They eat a lot in fall, and use the stored fat as a food source in winter.

▶ When winter comes and food is hard to find, hibernation will help the chipmunk make it through the winter.

Rabbits have two behaviours that help them survive in their habitats. If rabbits are frightened, they will "freeze" and sit very still. This helps them hide from danger in their natural habitat. If they have to hop away to escape danger, they go in a zigzag pattern that makes them harder to catch.

▶ Sitting very still, this rabbit may blend in with its habitat. This helps the rabbit avoid danger.

⇨ Check Your Understanding

1. Why do some birds feed in a group?

2. Explain one behaviour that helps animals adapt to the winter.

3. Why might you not see any animals if you went for a walk in a desert during the day?

Responses That Help Plants Adapt

Plants don't have behavioural adaptations the way animals do. They have responses to their habitats.

Plants respond to the changes in their habitats. Most plants stop growing over winter. Dormancy [DOR-muhn-see] is when something stops growing. Some trees lose their leaves in fall and grow new ones in spring. This helps them to save water over winter because they aren't losing it through their leaves. Other plants cannot survive the winter, but their seeds survive to start new plants in spring.

▲ When a seed sprouts, the root responds to the pull of gravity and grows down toward the soil.

▲ This tree loses its leaves to save water during the winter.

⇨ Check Your Understanding

1. Name two ways that plants respond to their habitats. How do these responses help plants?

Awesome SCIENCE

Amazing Adaptations

Warning Colours

Would you pet a black animal with a white stripe down its back? Probably not. The white stripe on a skunk is a warning sign that the skunk can produce a bad smell.

◀ The bold pattern on a skunk is a warning to other animals to stay away.

Animals that hide to protect themselves usually have colours that are dull and difficult to notice. But animals that taste bad, smell bad, or can sting often have bright colours or bold patterns that warn their enemies to stay away. The black and yellow stripes on a wasp warn that it can sting. The black and orange patterns on a Monarch butterfly warn birds that the butterfly tastes bad.

◀ Bright colours and a bold pattern on the Monarch butterfly are warning signs to enemies.

Mimicry

Some animals that are not dangerous have markings or body parts that make them look like an animal that is dangerous. This is called mimicry [MIM-ih-kree].

▲ A hover fly has stripes that make it look like a wasp, even though it cannot sting like a wasp.

▲ Colouring protects the good-tasting Viceroy butterfly by tricking birds into thinking it is a bad-tasting Monarch butterfly.

Some animals mimic the sound of other animals that are dangerous. A young burrowing owl will make a sound like a rattlesnake to try and scare coyotes, skunks, and squirrels away from its burrow.

Some animals have adaptations that make them look like plants.

▲ The insect in the photo above looks like a leaf!

Leaving Parts Behind

When a sea cucumber is attacked, it will vomit its insides out to cause a distraction. It can grow a new stomach later. When a salamander is grabbed, it can leave its tail behind in the mouth, hand, or paw of the attacker. It will grow a new tail later. These adaptations sound extreme, but they keep the animal alive.

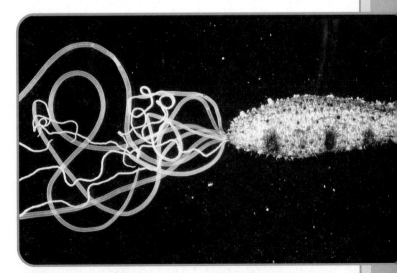

▲ A young burrowing owl can protect itself by making a sound like a rattlesnake.

▲ The sea cucumber causes a distraction to escape an attacker.

8 *What Lives Here?*

British Columbia has many different habitats. These habitats have different amounts of light and water, different types of food and soil, and different temperatures. Plants and animals live in the habitats that best meet their needs. Some of British Columbia's habitats and the organisms that live there are described below.

Boreal Forest Habitats

Much of the northern part of British Columbia is boreal [BOR-ee-uhl] forest. The winters are long and cold. The summers can be warm, but are very short. There are wet and dry areas, and trees that like each type of soil. There are many ponds and lakes within these forests. Moose, deer, bears, and wolves are common in this habitat.

▲ A boreal forest habitat has long winters, and many trees and lakes.

There are many moose in boreal forest habitats. Moose eat plants that grow near and under water. Ducks live on the ponds and lakes. In the forests, many birds eat the seeds of the black spruce tree. If deer are very hungry, they will also eat young black spruce trees.

▲ A boreal forest is a good habitat for moose, ducks, and black spruce trees.

Desert Habitats

Desert habitats in British Columbia are sunny and dry with sandy soil. Deserts are hot during the day and cold at night. Deserts have few trees. There are shrubs, clumps of grass, and small cacti. These plants have roots and leaves that help them live in the heat of a desert. These plants provide shelter from the Sun for some animals, and provide nesting sites or food for other animals.

▲ A desert habitat is sunny and dry.

The Great Basin pocket mouse lives only in a small desert area in British Columbia. The mouse likes to burrow in the sandy soil, where it will store and eat the seeds of the antelope brush shrub. Any seeds left uneaten will grow into shrubs the next year. Some caterpillars will eat only the leaves of the antelope brush.

▲ A desert is a good habitat for the Great Basin pocket mouse and antelope brush.

Temperate Rain Forest Habitats

There are rain forests along the coast of British Columbia. Rain forests have lots of rain, mist, or fog. The forests along the coast are temperate [TEM-puhr-iht], which means not too hot or too cold.

▲ A temperate rain forest is wet, green, and not too hot or too cold.

The moisture and cool temperature of a rain forest are good for plant growth. The many plants provide shade over streams, which makes the water cool. This makes streams a perfect habitat for fish like salmon. In the fall, the salmon lay their eggs in streams. The plants also help the fish hide from hungry eagles that nest in the tall trees above. Grizzly bears eat plants and salmon in some rain forests.

▲ A temperate rain forest is a good habitat for western hemlocks and red cedars, salmon, and grizzly bears.

⇨ Check Your Understanding

1. Which of the habitats described is most like the one where you live?

2. Which other habitats have you seen?

Chapter Review

Adaptations help organisms survive in their habitats.

Key Idea: Different habitats have different features.

Pond habitat   Desert habitat

Vocabulary
organism p. 153
habitat p. 153

Key Idea: Adaptations help organisms survive in different habitats.

Vocabulary
adaptation p. 163

Key Idea: Adaptations can be structures.

Key Idea: Adaptations can be behaviours or reponses.

Key Idea: Organisms live in habitats that have the conditions they need to grow and survive.

Review Key Ideas and Vocabulary

Use the vocabulary words in your answers to the questions.

1. Choose any two of the habitats described in this chapter. List the ways they are different from each other.

2. Look back at the picture of the sea otter at the beginning of this chapter. Draw a sea otter in the middle of your page. Reread the paragraphs about the sea otter. Label all the sea otter's adaptations on your picture. Put an S on the adaptations that are structures, and a B on behaviours.

thick fur

3. Copy the table below into your notebook. In the first column, draw three adaptations that help plants get more sunlight. In the second column, draw three adaptations that help plants survive with little water.

Adaptations that help plants get more sunlight	Adaptations that help plants survive with little water

4. List four adaptations that help animals survive seasonal changes. Name an animal with each adaptation.

5. Look at this photo of an aquarium habitat. Explain how this aquarium setup provides light, water, an appropriate temperature range, food, and shelter for the plants and animals that are living in it.

Apply What You've Learned

Make Organism Cards

Looking Back

You have learned

- about the ways that habitats can differ
- about the adaptations that help organisms survive in their habitats
- that organisms live in habitats with conditions they need to grow and survive

Have you seen baseball or hockey cards? They have photos of a player on the front, and information about the player on the back. In this activity, you will make an organism card for an organism that lives in a British Columbia habitat.

Demonstrate Your Learning

Organism Cards

1. Your organism can be a plant or an animal. If you choose an animal, it must be a wild animal, not a pet. It can live near you or somewhere else, but it must be from British Columbia. You might need to do some research to choose an organism.

2. Use books or the Internet or both to find information about the organism you chose. Ask Aboriginal Elders or local naturalists what they know about your organism.

3. Take notes in your notebook. Note the name of the area where your organism lives. Note details of the organism's habitat. If it is a plant, you might write about whether it grows in sunshine or shade, if it needs a lot of water to grow, and so on. If it is an animal, you can write about the food it eats, where it finds shelter, and so on. Note the adaptations that help it grow and survive in this habitat. Identify which adaptations are structures and which are behaviours or responses.

4. Now, make your organism card. The front of the card should have a picture of your organism and its name. Try to include some details about the organism's habitat in your picture if you can. You can draw the picture, print one from the Internet, or cut one out of a magazine. (Be sure to have your teacher's or a parent's permission first!)

   The back of your card should have a description of your organism's habitat and information about its adaptations.

⇨ Assessment Checklist

ORGANISM CARD

As you create your organism card, make sure that you show you are able to

✔ describe the habitat of your organism in terms of
  - light
  - water
  - temperature
  - food
  - shelter

✔ identify your organism's adaptations

✔ distinguish between different adaptations

Living things get food from their habitats.

⇨ **Key Ideas**

▸ Habitats contain communities of living things.

▸ Plants use sunlight to make food.

▸ Animals eat plants or other animals for food.

▸ Food chains show who eats whom.

▸ A change to one part of a food chain affects other parts.

▸ Food webs are made of food chains.

All living things need food. This moose is a large animal. It gets what it needs to grow and survive by eating plants that live in its habitat. Where do plants get their food? Are there other animals in this habitat that get their food by eating the moose?

In this chapter, you will learn about how organisms get food from their habitats.

Populations and Communities

◀ A pond community is made up of populations of plants and animals.

All the members of one type of plant or animal in a habitat are called a **population** [POP-yuh-LAY-shun]. All the cattails (a water plant) in this pond are a population. All the ducks in this pond are a population. All the mosquitoes that live in and around this pond are a population. Coyotes that feed on pond animals are a population.

When two or more populations live in the same habitat, they form a **community** [kuh-MYOO-nih-tee]. The pond community in the photo is made up of several populations.

Plant and animal populations that make up a community depend on each other for different things. Plants can provide shelter and food for animals.

> ⇨ **Learning Tip**
>
> Make connections to other things you have learned about in school. Have you learned about populations or communities in Social Studies?

⇨ Check Your Understanding

1. Are the tadpoles in a pond a population or a community?
2. Name five populations of plants and five populations of animals that share your community.

2 How Plants and Animals Get Food

All living things need food. They get their food from their habitat. A population can only live in a habitat if the habitat has the food the population needs. In a community, some populations of living things eat other populations of living things. Think back to the pond community—ducks eat water plants and mosquito larvae [LAHR-vee]. Coyotes eat ducks.

Living things get their food in one of two ways. They either produce their own food or they eat other organisms for food.

Producers

Plants produce their own food using sunlight, water from the soil, and carbon dioxide from the air. We call plants **producers.**

▲ Algae [AL-jee] are producers.

▲ Trees are producers.

Consumers

Animals cannot make their own food. They eat plants or other animals to get food. We call animals **consumers** because they consume food.

Animals that eat only plants are called **herbivores** [HUR-buh-vorz].

▲ Beavers are herbivores because they eat only plants.

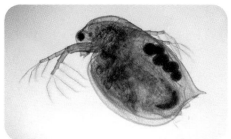

▲ Daphnia [DAF-nee-uh] are herbivores because they eat algae.

Animals that eat other animals are called **carnivores** [CAR-nuh-vorz].

▲ A wolf is a carnivore because it eats deer.

▲ A frog is a carnivore because it eats insects and shrimp.

Animals that eat both plants and animals are called **omnivores** [AHM-nuh-vorz].

▲ A grizzly bear is an omnivore because it eats salmon and many types of plants.

▲ A duck is an omnivore because it eats both water plants and small animals like Daphnia.

Some animals eat animals that are dying or already dead. They are called **scavengers.** Scavengers are carnivores because they eat other animals.

▲ Crows eat animals that are killed by passing cars and trucks on some highways.

Classify Living Things

Skills Focus: classifying

1. Work with a partner. Look at the sketches below. What types of food does each organism on the left use? Is each organism a producer, herbivore, carnivore, omnivore, or scavenger? Some organisms may fit into more than one category.

2. Write your answers in your notebook. Compare your answers with another pair of students.

Grizzly bear   eats   Grasses   Skunk cabbage   Red elderberry   Salmon

Hare   eats   Strawberry plant   Fireweed plant   Parts of many trees

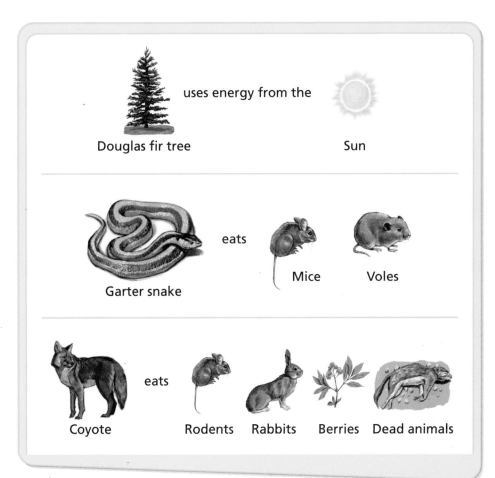

Douglas fir tree   uses energy from the   Sun

Garter snake   eats   Mice   Voles

Coyote   eats   Rodents   Rabbits   Berries   Dead animals

⇨ Check Your Understanding

1. What three things do plants need to make their own food?

2. In your notebook, make a table like the one below. List what each consumer eats, and give two examples of each consumer.

	What does this consumer eat?	Give two examples of this consumer.
Herbivore		
Carnivore		
Omnivore		
Scavenger		

3. What type of consumer are you?

⇨ Learning Tip

Locate the information you need to fill in this table by scanning the section for vocabulary words and photos.

3 Food Chains

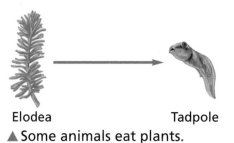

Elodea   Tadpole

▲ Some animals eat plants.

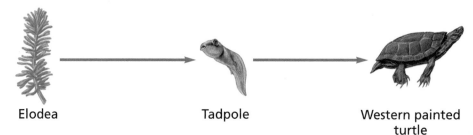

Elodea   Tadpole   Western painted
                                                        turtle

▲ Some animals eat an animal that has eaten a plant.

These diagrams show **food chains.** They show who eats whom in a community. When a plant or animal is eaten, energy passes from the plant or animal to the consumer.

In the second chain above, Elodea [ih-LO-dee-uh] uses energy from the Sun to make food. Tadpoles eat Elodea to get energy they need to survive. Energy has passed from Elodea to the tadpoles. Turtles then eat tadpoles. Energy has passed from Elodea to the tadpoles to the turtle.

Some food chains have more than two or three steps. Humans can also be part of food chains.

Humans are part of a food chain with grass and cows. Grass uses energy from the Sun to make food. When cows eat grass, energy passes from the grass to the cow. When we drink milk or eat meat from the cow, the energy is passed from the cow to us.

Learning Tip

Check your understanding by sketching the food chain described in the last paragraph.

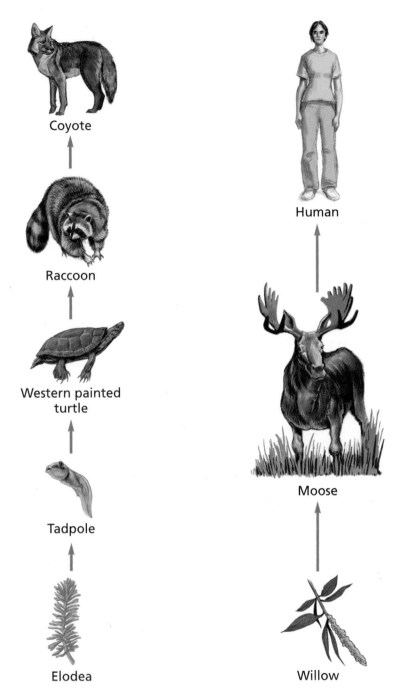

Coyote

Raccoon

Western painted turtle

Tadpole

Elodea

Human

Moose

Willow

▲ Food chains show who eats whom in a habitat.

⇨ Check Your Understanding

1. Draw a food chain for a pet bird that eats sunflower seeds. Be sure to identify the producers and consumers in the food chain.
2. Draw a food chain to show that ice cream starts with the Sun.

4 Changes in Food Chains

What happens when one of the links in a bicycle chain is removed? The bicycle no longer works. The same thing can happen to a food chain. If a plant or animal population is missing from the food chain, then other parts of the chain are affected.

Try This: Break a Food Chain

Skills Focus: classifying, observing, interpreting data

Look at the following food chain.

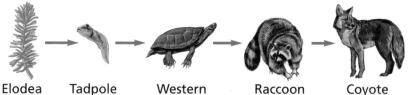

Elodea   Tadpole   Western painted turtle   Raccoon   Coyote

1. Form groups of five and give each person one of the roles in the food chain: Elodea, tadpole, turtle, raccoon, and coyote.

2. Use lengths of string or yarn to connect yourselves in the food chain shown above.

3. If there were no tadpoles, what would happen to the food chain? To find out, have the tadpole person drop their strings.

4. If there were no tadpoles, what would happen to the turtles? Animals that eat the tadpoles should drop their string. Continue the activity by asking what would happen if there were no turtles. What would happen if there were no raccoons? What do you think would happen to the Elodea without any tadpoles? What has happened to the food chain?

The Try This activity showed that every organism in a food chain is very important to every other organism in the chain. If one organism disappears from a food chain, the other organisms may go hungry and die. A population does not have to disappear to affect a food chain. Sometimes a change in the size of a population can affect a food chain.

Predators and Prey

Animals that hunt other animals for food are called predators. The food a predator hunts is called its prey. The populations of predator and prey can have important effects on each other.

The sea otter is a predator. An important prey of the sea otter is the sea urchin.

▲ A sea otter eating a sea urchin

Sea urchins eat large seaweed called kelp. Kelp can reach from the ocean floor up to the surface of the ocean. Many kelp plants make a kelp forest. Kelp forests provide food and shelter for a number of organisms, including sea otters.

▲ A kelp forest

The food chain in this habitat looks like this:

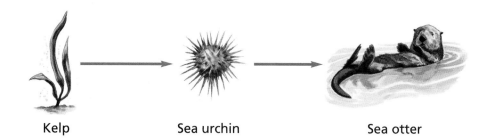

Kelp   Sea urchin   Sea otter

▶ This food chain shows how the sea otter gets some of its food.

Until the late 1700s, there were many sea otters along the Pacific coast from northern Mexico to Alaska. People hunted the otters for their fur, and by 1910 there were very few otters left. The hunting of sea otters has now stopped and the number of sea otters is going up.

In places where there are many sea otters, there are few urchins because the otters eat them. Because there are few sea urchins to eat the kelp, there is lots of kelp.

⬥ Learning Tip

Connect this graph to what you just read. Ask yourself, "Why is this graph included? What information does it give me?"

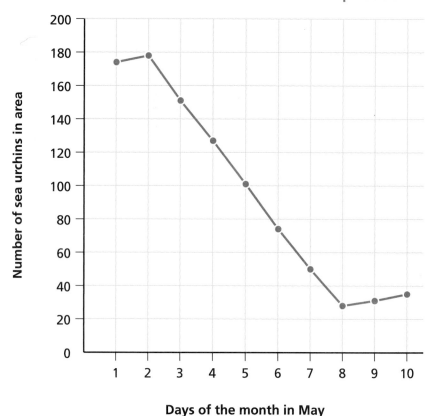

**Predators and Prey:
How One Sea Otter Can Affect a Sea Urchin Population**

Number of sea urchins in area

Days of the month in May

In places where there are few sea otters, there are many sea urchins. Sea urchins eat kelp. If a community has very few sea otters, there are many sea urchins feeding on kelp. What happens to the kelp forest if there are too many sea urchins in one area? The kelp forest is destroyed by sea urchins. This means that the good habitat for many ocean creatures is destroyed.

Studying Changes in Food Chains

When scientists study communities, they look at the predator populations and the prey populations. They are interested in seeing how a change in one part of the food chain will affect these populations. Scientists often work with Aboriginal groups who have lived in the area for many generations. The Aboriginal people can tell the scientists how populations of different organisms have changed over time.

Learning Tip

Pause and think. Ask yourself, "What did I just read? What did it mean?" Then try to put it in your own words.

Check Your Understanding

1. Give an example of a predator and its prey.
2. Look at the food chain below. What would happen to the number of termites if there were more owls to eat the voles?

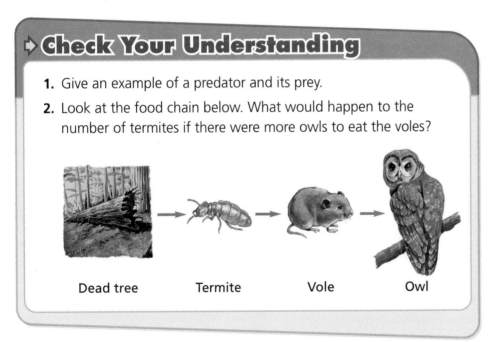

| Dead tree | Termite | Vole | Owl |

5 Food Webs Are Made of Food Chains

Build a Pond Food Web

Skills Focus: communicating

1. Work in a small group. Cut a piece of letter-size paper lengthwise into five equal strips. Then, fold each strip of paper to make four "boxes."

2. Draw the following pond habitat food chains on the strips of paper, with one organism in each box. Tear off any extra boxes. If a chain has more than four steps, tape an extra box onto the strip.
   Elodea—tadpole—turtle—raccoon
   Elodea—duck—coyote
   algae—clam—raccoon
   algae—Daphnia—duck
   algae—shrimp—dragonfly larva—duck—coyote

3. Arrange the food chains on your desk so that same animals overlap. How would you describe the pattern you made? (Note: You may have to fold some chains to make this work.)

Plants and animals can be part of more than one food chain because many consumers eat more than one type of food. In the Try This activity, Elodea was part of two different food chains. Food chains can be linked together to form a **food web.** A food web can show how producers, consumers, and scavengers are connected in a habitat. Food webs help us understand how complicated habitats are.

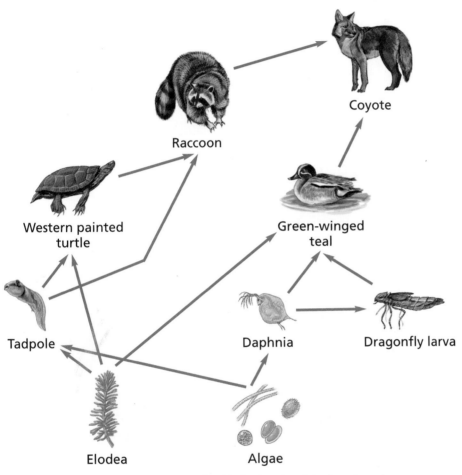

Raccoon

Coyote

Western painted turtle

Green-winged teal

Tadpole

Daphnia

Dragonfly larva

Elodea

Algae

▲ Use your finger to trace the food chains in this food web.

> **Learning Tip**
>
> Examine this food web diagram carefully. Use your finger to trace each food chain. Remember to always start with a producer.

⇨ Check Your Understanding

1. What does a food web show that a food chain does not?
2. The pond food web above shows only some of the living things in the pond. What do you think the food web would look like if all the organisms in the habitat were included?

Chapter Review

Living things get food from their habitats.

Key Idea: Habitats contain communities of living things.

Vocabulary
population p. 183
community p. 183

Key Idea: Plants use sunlight to make food.

Vocabulary
producer p. 184

Key Idea: Animals eat plants or other animals for food.

Herbivore　　Carnivore　　Omnivore　　Scavenger

Consumers

Vocabulary
consumer p. 185
herbivore p. 185
carnivore p. 185
omnivore p. 185
scavenger p. 186

Key Idea: Food chains show who eats whom.

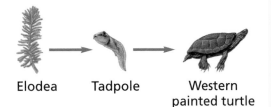

Elodea   Tadpole   Western painted turtle

Vocabulary
food chain p. 188

Key Idea: A change to one part of a food chain affects other parts.

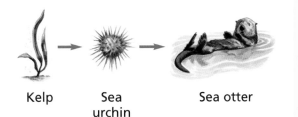

Kelp   Sea urchin   Sea otter

Vocabulary
predator p. 191
prey p. 191

Key Idea: Food webs are made of food chains.

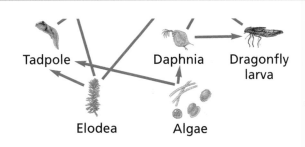

Tadpole   Daphnia   Dragonfly larva

Elodea   Algae

Vocabulary
food web p. 195

Review Key Ideas and Vocabulary

Use the vocabulary words in your answers to the questions.

1. What is the difference between a population and a community?

2. How do plants get food?

3. How do animals get food?

4. Draw and label a food chain that includes a producer, a herbivore, and a carnivore.

5. What would happen to the herbivores and carnivores in your food chain if the producers disappeared?

6. Why do we combine food chains into food webs?

Local Habitat Food Chains

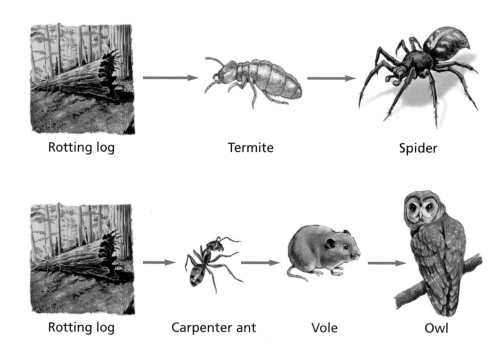

Rotting log → Termite → Spider

Rotting log → Carpenter ant → Vole → Owl

▲ Think about your local habitat. You might look at a small habitat within a larger habitat. These food chains were created using a rotting log habitat. The rotting log habitat is found in a forest habitat.

Looking Back

You have learned

- that food chains start with energy from the Sun
- that plants can use sunlight to make their own food
- that animals must eat plants and other animals for food
- how to use food chains to show who eats whom

Demonstrate Your Learning

Choose Your Animal

1. Work as a class to brainstorm a list of animals in your local habitat. Choose one animal to study. Find out what that animal eats and what eats it. Is it a herbivore, carnivore, omnivore, or scavenger?

Draw Your Food Chain

1. Draw a diagram of a food chain that includes your animal.

2. Post your food chain on a bulletin board labelled "Food Chains in Our Local Habitat."

⇨ Assessment Checklist

LOCAL HABITAT FOOD CHAIN

As you make your local habitat food chain, make sure that you show you are able to

- ✔ identify producers and consumers
- ✔ identify and distinguish between herbivores, carnivores, omnivores, and scavengers
- ✔ accurately identify which organisms eat other organisms

Chapter 10

Personal choices affect habitats and communities.

Key Ideas

▸ Human actions have an impact on habitats.

▸ Changes in a habitat can affect the survival of a population.

▸ People can conserve habitats.

▸ Personal choices can have a positive or a negative effect on habitats.

▸ Traditional Aboriginal cultures show respect for habitats and communities.

Each of these pictures tells a different story about personal choice. Where did the beach garbage come from? What choices did people make to create the problems in the first photo? How might their attitude about Earth be different from the people in the second photo? What personal choices did people in the second photo make? How is their choice helping Earth?

In this chapter, you will learn how personal choices can affect habitats and communities.

Human Actions Affect Habitats

People cause many changes to habitats. People change habitats when they build roads and houses.

▲ How was this habitat changed by people? How did these changes affect plants and animals in this habitat?

Aboriginal peoples sometimes change habitats by burning off sections of land. This helps some food plants, such as camas bulbs, grow larger.

→ Learning Tip

There is a question under each of the photos in this section. Compare your answers with the answers of another student.

▲ How would burning this field of camas affect plants and animals in this habitat?

People change habitats when they fish or farm to produce food.

▲ How was this habitat changed by farmers adding water to the land? How did these changes affect plants and animals in this habitat?

People change habitats when they produce energy such as electricity [ih-lehk-TRIS-ih-tee].

◄ People build dams and flood large areas to produce electricity. How did these changes affect plants and animals in this habitat?

People change habitats with the garbage and waste they produce.

▲ How are these land and water habitats being changed by garbage and waste? How did these changes affect plants and animals in this habitat?

People even change habitats when they play!

▲ How did building a tree house affect plants and animals in this habitat?

Observe Human Changes to Habitats

Skills Focus: observing, inferring

1. Go for a walk in the neighbourhood near your school.

2. Draw a picture or write a description of what the habitat looked like before people changed it. What plants and animals might have been there that are not there now? What plants and animals might have been added to the neighbourhood?

⇨ Check Your Understanding

1. List or draw some ways that people change habitats. Put an asterisk (*) beside the changes you have seen near where you live.

chapter 70

The Effects of Changes in Habitats

Some changes to habitats are caused by people and some are natural. Natural changes include forest fires, avalanches, tornadoes, hurricanes, and other types of storms.

▲ The forest on the left was destroyed when the trees were cut down by people. The forest on the right was destroyed by a fire started by lightning. What do you think happened to the plants and animals that lived in these forests?

Any change in a habitat can affect the communities of plants and animals that live in that habitat. Some organisms are no longer able to find what they need to survive. Plants may die. Sometimes, a different type of plant grows instead. Animals move away or die. Sometimes, different animals move into a habitat to replace animals no longer living in that habitat.

If negative changes happen to a habitat, it may put plant and animal populations in danger. Scientists say that these plants and animals are **threatened.**

If a habitat changes a lot, some populations of plants and animals can be in danger of disappearing forever. Scientists say that these plants and animals are **endangered.** Organisms that are threatened may become endangered if the things that put the organisms in danger are not stopped.

Why Organisms Become Endangered

Some animals are threatened or endangered because they can no longer find shelter in their habitats. Shelter is destroyed when cities, farms, and roads are built.

▲ Cities and farming mean fewer places for badgers to dig burrows. Burrowing owls depend on holes made by badgers for homes.

▲ The white-tailed jackrabbit has less to eat because cattle are eating some of its food.

Some animals are threatened or endangered because they have to compete for food with new animals that people have brought into the habitat. New animals may eat organisms already in the habitat.

Some plants and animals are threatened or endangered because they are killed by things that people put into habitats. Chemicals can harm water, air, and soil that living things need to survive.

▲ The Viceroy butterfly population is endangered because chemicals used in orchards kill the butterflies.

▲ Pallid bats move away when disturbed by hikers and rock climbers.

Some animals do not like to be disturbed by humans. These animals will move out of a habitat if people disturb them.

Plants and animals can also become threatened or endangered when too many of them are taken out of the habitat. There are laws about how many fish people can catch, which animals people can hunt, and where plants can be picked. These laws help protect plant and animal populations.

▲ It is illegal to take abalone [AB-uh-LO-NEE] from the ocean today because too many were taken by divers years ago. The Huu-ay-aht First Nation near Bamfield is trying to restore the abalone population.

When a plant or animal does disappear from Earth, we say it has become **extinct.** Dinosaurs became extinct millions of years ago. Organisms are still becoming extinct today.

Did you know?

Five animals from British Columbia have become extinct in the last 100 years. The Dawson caribou from Haida Gwaii [HY-duh G-why] became extinct in 1908. The Dragon Lake whitefish became extinct in 1956 when a chemical was used to make Dragon Lake, near Quesnel, better for fishing. Two kinds of stickleback became extinct in the early 1990s when catfish that were put in Hadley Lake on Lasqueti Island ate them all. The passenger pigeon became extinct in 1914. The photo below is a stuffed passenger pigeon from a museum.

⇨ Check Your Understanding

1. List five reasons why a plant or animal might become endangered.
2. Give two examples of animals that are extinct.

③ Conservation

People need food, energy, and places to live. Many people want to find ways to get what they need without harming habitats.

Human actions can cause changes to habitats. These changes can threaten or endanger plants and animals in the habitat. When people make plans to stop any further damage to habitats, it is called **conservation** [KON-sur-VAY-shun].

Here are some ways that people are working to conserve habitats.

▶ A few areas of natural habitat can be conserved in a city.

▶ Logging companies can leave some areas with trees so that animals have shelter as they move from area to area.

◀ The Nuu-chah-nulth First Nation and the West Coast Vancouver Island Aquatic Management Board work together to monitor and protect the water resources and habitats in the Checleset Bay Ecological Reserve.

Please Stay on the Trail

Do not enter this sensitive habitat

Thank You

Massachusetts Audubon Society

◀ Hiking only on the trails helps conserve this forest habitat.

Conservation is a positive way that people can affect habitats. Conservation of habitats means that Earth will be better able to provide clean air and water for all living things.

▷ Check Your Understanding

1. Why do people have conservation plans for habitats?
2. Give one example of the conservation of a habitat near where you live. How would the habitat change if there were no conservation plan?

Tech·CONNECT

Jackets from Pop Bottles

PETE

Have you ever worn a fleece jacket? Have you ever slept in a sleeping bag? Did you know that the fleece in the jacket and the stuffing in the sleeping bag can be made of recycled plastic pop bottles?

Pop bottles are collected from recycling programs, like blue boxes. Pop bottles and other products similar to pop bottles, such as peanut butter containers and cooking oil bottles, are separated from other types of plastic. These types of containers have a symbol on them like the one to the left. These bottles and containers are then sent to a recycling plant.

First the pop bottles are sorted by colour. Then the bottles are crushed and chopped into small plastic flakes. The flakes are washed and dried to get rid of any dirt or paper labels. The plastic flakes are then melted and formed into plastic fibres or pellets.

▲ Crushed bottles

▲ Bottles being chopped

▲ Flakes being washed

210

The plastic fibres are then woven to make yarn, which can be used to make fabric. This fabric is sold to clothing companies that use the fabric to make jackets, hats, scarves, and mitts. It takes about 25 2-L pop bottles to make each medium-sized adult jacket. The fibres can also be used to make carpets, blankets, or stuffing for jackets and sleeping bags. It takes about 85 2-L pop bottles to make enough stuffing for one sleeping bag.

▲ Plastic fibres like these go into fleece jackets and sleeping bags.

The plastic pellets can be used to make new plastic products such as bottles, key chains, buckets, lawn furniture, and garbage bags. Recycled pop bottles can even be used to make new blue boxes for recycling more pop bottles!

▲ Plastic pellets like these are used to make new bottles and lawn furniture.

Personal Choices Affect Habitats

People make choices that affect habitats. A choice may harm habitats or help conserve habitats. People of all ages can make choices that will help conserve habitats. Many times during the day, you make choices that affect habitats.

▲ How do these personal choices affect habitats?

▲ How did someone's personal choice cause trouble for this bird?

Littering

Keeping garbage in its place helps prevent changes to habitats. Animals sometimes eat litter, as they try to get bits of food from a package. This can make the animals very sick, or even kill them. Garbage also attracts scavengers. Once scavengers enter an area, they often find and eat baby animals.

Food Packaging

The packaging from many food products usually ends up in the garbage. If we have less garbage we will not need to change as many natural habitats into landfills or garbage dumps. Eating fresh, unpackaged foods is one way of using less packaging.

▲ Compare the garbage from each snack.

Taking your lunch to school in reuseable containers reduces the amount of garbage produced. Using a lunch box means that there is no bag to throw out.

Eating fewer prepared foods is also a way of using less electricity.

▲ Many people take their lunch in reuseable plastic containers. There is no garbage.

▲ Prepared foods are made in factories, which use a lot of electricity.

Recycling

Many towns and cities have places to bring your newspapers, cardboard, tins, and clear glass. These items can be used again to make more of the same thing.

▲ Used glass jars are broken, heated, and made into new jars.

Using Less Electricity

When you enter a room, do you turn on a light? When you leave the room, do you turn it off? Do you turn off your computer when you are not using it? Electricity is produced by human-made dams. Building these dams changes many habitats. Using less electricity means that fewer dams will need to be built. This can help conserve habitats.

▲ You use less electricity if you turn off lights and use energy-saving light bulbs. If you use less electricity, fewer habitats have to be changed to produce it.

Driving

Walking, biking, taking the bus, or car pooling are ways to use less gasoline. Gasoline [GAS-uh-LEEN] is made from oil, which is taken out of the ground. Taking oil out of the ground changes the habitat. Then large factories called oil refineries make gasoline for cars.

▲ How might the habitat have been changed by this oil refinery?

Using a car also puts harmful parts of gasoline into the air. This is the air that plants and animals, including humans, need to survive.

⭷ Learning Tip

React to what you read by giving your opinion. Do you think people should drive less? Why or why not?

⭷ Check Your Understanding

1. How does turning off a light help conserve habitats?
2. How do families that live without electricity or a car help conserve habitats?
3. How can you help reduce the garbage you make with your school lunch?

Traditional Aboriginal Cultures and Habitats

▲ This meal of food from the wild is healthier for you than many meals that are common today. Can you identify these foods?

▲ The bark of this cedar tree will be used for making mats, baskets, and hats. The tree will continue to grow because only a narrow strip of bark is removed.

The tradition of Aboriginal peoples of British Columbia is to care for the natural foods in habitats that surround them. They clip berry bushes so the plants will continue to make berries. Many Aboriginal peoples gather only as much plant life as they need. This way, there are plants available to use in later years. Other plants are replanted to make sure that a habitat stays healthy. Aboriginal cultures have survived for thousands of years because of their awareness of and respect for the habitats and communities around them.

Working together, Aboriginal peoples and scientists are making a difference for the endangered plants and animals in British Columbia. Aboriginal peoples have observed and cared for the land they live on and its plants and animals for many generations. This knowledge has been passed on in stories and songs. Over time, they have seen many changes.

Scientists are paying more attention to the knowledge of Aboriginal cultures. They are now working with Aboriginal peoples to learn how habitats are changing. With help from Aboriginal peoples, scientists are learning which animals have moved to different places, how the number of birds has changed, and that ice is melting sooner in the spring.

▲ The Sliammon First Nation and the owners of a pulp mill worked together to install a machine to add more water to the Theodosia River. More water in the river has helped the salmon habitat.

◀ The Nk'mip [in-ka-meep] Desert and Heritage Centre teaches people about the endangered desert habitat and how Aboriginal peoples live there. This metal cut out shows an Aboriginal woman harvesting bitterroot.

⇨ Check Your Understanding

1. How do Aboriginal peoples show respect for plants?
2. What are scientists learning from Aboriginal peoples?

ScienceWorks

A'qam Native Plant Nursery

The St. Mary's Indian Band is part of the Ktunaxa [k-too-nah-ha] Nation. The St. Mary's band is known as A'qam [ah-kam], or "people of the dense forest or brush" in the Ktunaxa language. A'qam has been their home for thousands of years.

▲ The A'qam Native Plant Nursery is located just outside Cranbrook, British Columbia.

The St. Mary's Indian Band has started a business that helps local habitats and animals. The band has a nursery where they grow plants native to British Columbia. Native plants are plants that grow naturally in a certain area. Many plants that you can buy from a nursery are not actually from British Columbia. When native plants are used, wild animals have more seeds and berries to eat. The native plants use less water and fertilizer. This is because the native plants have adapted to living in the habitat.

The nursery was started when a power line was put through part of the Ktunaxa Nation's land. A strip of land had been cleared under the power line, and the power company was going to use its regular seed mix to replant the area. This seed mix was made of seeds of plants that are not native to British Columbia. Members of the Ktunaxa Nation wanted to replant with plants native to the area. The Ktunaxa Nation felt that using native grasses and shrubs would be easier on the soil. It would also be better for local wildlife and mean fewer weeds.

The power company agreed and the St. Mary's Indian Band started the A'qam Native Plant Nursery. When the nursery started in 2000, it was only one building. Today, there are five buildings and the band grows about 30 different kinds of plants native to British Columbia.

▲ This band member is caring for plants in the nursery.

Chapter 10

Chapter Review

Personal choices affect habitats and communities.

Key Idea: Human actions have an impact on habitats.

Key Idea: Changes in a habitat can affect the survival of a population.

Vocabulary
threatened p. 204
endangered p. 205
extinct p. 207

Key Idea: People can conserve habitats.

Vocabulary
conservation p. 208

Key Idea: Personal choices can have a positive or a negative effect on habitats.

Positive

Negative

Key Idea: Traditional Aboriginal cultures show respect for habitats and communities.

Review Key Ideas and Vocabulary

Use the vocabulary words in your answers to the questions.

1. Give three examples of ways that a habitat can be changed. In each case, say whether it is a natural change or one caused by people.

2. Describe three ways people can conserve habitats.

3. Give an example of a personal choice you could make that could have a positive effect on your habitat. Give an example of a personal choice that could have a negative effect on your habitat.

4. Why do scientists who study habitats want to work with local Aboriginal groups?

Apply What You've Learned

A Personal Choice

Looking Back

You have learned

- that people's choices and actions can affect habitats
- that changes to habitats can threaten or endanger populations of plants and animals
- that people can make conservation plans and personal choices that limit the changes to natural habitats
- about some ways that Aboriginal peoples respect habitats

Demonstrate Your Learning

Make a Choice

1. In this activity, you will make a personal choice that will have a positive effect on your habitat.

2. Make a poster or pamphlet, or give a short speech, to convince other students to make the same personal choice. You may also want to try to convince adults, such as relatives or neighbours, to make the same choice.

⇨ Assessment Checklist

PERSONAL CHOICE

As you make your poster, pamphlet, or speech, make sure that you show you are able to

✔ clearly state your personal choice
✔ explain how it will be good for your habitat
✔ explain how your personal choice might affect the plants and animals that live in the habitat

Making Connections

Help a Habitat

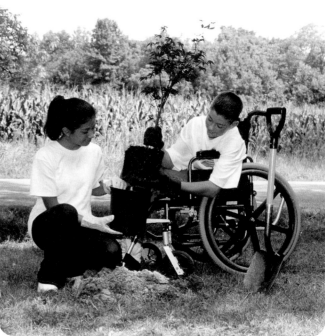

Looking Back

In this unit, you have learned
- that different habitats have different features
- that the personal choices you make affect habitats

Now you will work on a class project to help a local habitat.

Demonstrate Your Learning

1. **Identify a local habitat.** Think of a local habitat. This can be your schoolyard, or it can be a nearby shoreline, stream, or green space.

2. **Choose your task.** How could you help care for this habitat? Be sure to consider
   - what living things use this habitat
   - food chains and food webs in this habitat
   - how people are affecting living things in this habitat

3. **Check for success.** How will you know if your project was successful?

4. **Gather information.** Make a list of the questions you would like answered. You can research using a local naturalist club, libraries, or the Internet. You can talk to local Aboriginal groups or naturalists.

5. **Plan.** Make a list of steps. Decide when you will work on each step. You may need to get permission to do certain things. List all of the materials you may need, and where you will get them. Think carefully about how your plan will affect the living things in the habitat.

6. **Get to work.** Try out your habitat care project.

7. **Evaluate.** Were you able to care for a local habitat? Did you check for success? Would you change anything to improve your project?

8. **Communicate.** To complete your task, make a presentation or take action. Share your project with your classmates, your community, local businesses, or local organizations.

> ⇨ **Assessment Checklist**

HELP A HABITAT

Check to make sure that your work shows that you can

- ✔ identify organisms in the habitat
- ✔ identify the needs of the organisms in the habitat
- ✔ identify the relationships among organisms in the habitat
- ✔ identify actions that would have a positive effect on the habitat
- ✔ evaluate the effect of your actions on the habitat

Science Safety Rules

- ## Follow your teacher's directions.

Always follow your teacher's instructions. Ask your teacher for help if you're not sure what to do. Wear safety goggles or other safety equipment that your teacher tells you to wear.

- ## Tell your teacher about any problems.

Tell your teacher immediately if you see a safety hazard, such as broken glass or a spill. Also tell your teacher if you see another student doing something you think is dangerous. Tell your teacher about any allergies or medical problems you have.

- ## Be clean and tidy.

Keep yourself and your work area tidy and clean. Clean up and put away equipment after you have finished. Wash your hands carefully with soap and water at the end of each activity.

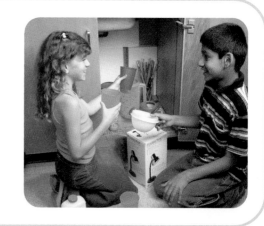

Heat and Fire

- Keep yourself and anything else that can burn away from heat or flames.
- Never touch an object that has been heated. Slowly bring the back of your hand toward the object until you are sure it is not hot.

Chemicals

- Never put your nose directly over a chemical to smell it. Gently wave your hand over the chemical until you can smell the fumes.
- Wash your hands well after handling chemicals.

Handle with Care

Glass and Sharp Objects

- Handle glassware, knives, and other sharp instruments with care.
- Never point a knife or sharp object at another person.
- Tell your teacher immediately if you break glassware or cut yourself.

Living Things

- Treat all living things with care and respect.
- Never hurt an animal in any way.
- Always wash your hands with soap after touching plants or animals.

Measuring

Measuring is an important part of doing science. Measurements allow you to give exact information when you are describing something.

Measuring Length

You measure length when you want to find out how long something is. You also measure length when you want to know how deep, how tall, how far, or how wide something is. The metre (m) is the basic unit of length.

> Length is the distance between two points. Four units can be used to measure length: metres (m), centimetres (cm), millimetres (mm), and kilometres (km).
>
> 1000 mm = 1 m   100 cm = 1 m   1000 m = 1 km

Metric ruler

Tape measure

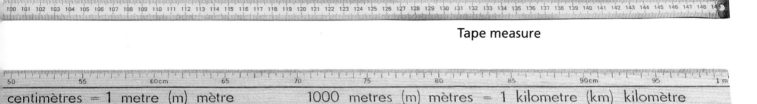

centimètres = 1 metre (m) mètre   1000 metres (m) mètres = 1 kilometre (km) kilomètre

Metre stick

▲ Which of these measuring tools would you use to measure your height? Which would you use to measure the size of your waist? Which would you use to measure the width of your notebook?

Measuring Liquid Volume

You measure volume when you want to measure the amount of liquid in a container. Scientists use special containers, with measurements marked on them, so that they can get precise measures of volume.

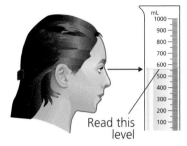

> Volume is the amount of space something takes up. Liquid volume is measured in litres (L) and millilitres (mL).
>
> 1000 mL = 1 L

▲ To read the measurement of a liquid correctly, make sure your eyes are at the same level as the top of the liquid.

Measuring Temperature

> Temperature tells us how hot or cold something is. In science, temperature is measured in degrees Celsius (°C).
>
> 0 °C = freezing point of water
> 20 °C = room temperature
> 37.6 °C = normal body temperature
> 100 °C = boiling point of water

There are many different kinds of thermometers, and many work the same way. When the liquid in the thermometer gets warmer, it takes up more space and rises up the tube. When the liquid gets cooler, it shrinks and the liquid goes down. The numbers on thermometers are called the scale. To find the temperature, you read the number on the scale that is at the same height as the liquid.

▲ Hold the thermometer at eye level to be sure your reading is accurate.

Reading for Information

Reading Tips

When you are reading a science textbook, you are reading for information. Reading for information takes some special skills you don't use when you read a story. Here are some tips to help you read.

Before Reading

Look at the pictures and the headings. Ask yourself what the section is going to be about. Think about what you already know about the topic. What else would you like to find out? Write your ideas and questions before you start reading.

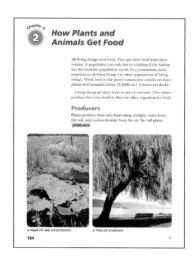

During Reading

Stop and think as you read. Sometimes, you may need to read a part again. Check to make sure you understand. Notice the important science words. Remember, you can use the glossary or study the pictures to help you understand the words. Spend time on the pictures and tables as well as on the words.

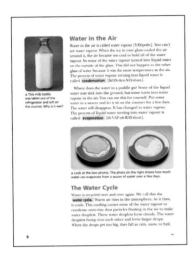

After Reading

Ask yourself: What did I learn? What's most important for me to remember? How does this information fit in with other things I already know about? Then, answer the questions at the end of a section. These questions will help you check your understanding of what you read. They will help you make connections to other science topics, to your own life, and to events in Canada and the world.

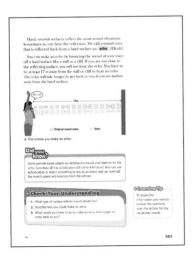

Using Graphic Organizers

Sometimes it is helpful to use a picture or a chart to show what you are thinking. You can read the information in the picture or in the chart just like you read text on a page.

▶ A **word web** shows a main idea in the centre of the web with related ideas around it.

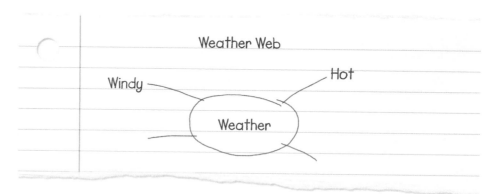

▶ A **KWL chart** shows what you Know about a topic, what you Wonder, and what you have Learned about the topic.

Know	Wonder	Learned
There are many sources of light	Are light sources natural or artificial?	The Sun is a natural source of light

▶ A food chain is a type of **flow chart**. It shows a sequence of steps.

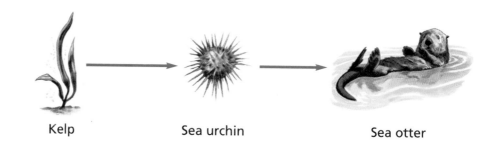

Kelp   Sea urchin   Sea otter

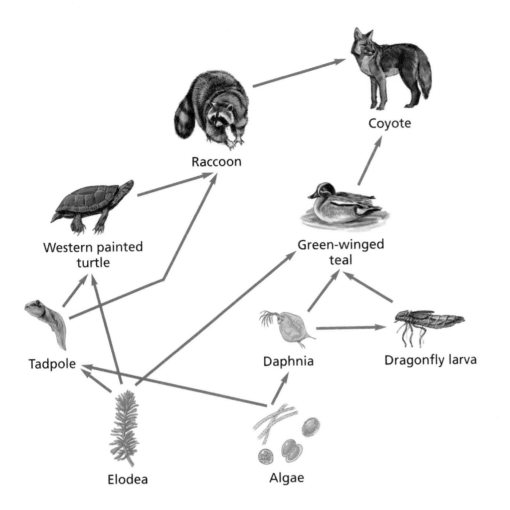

◀ A **concept map** shows a collection of words or pictures or both.

Raccoon

Coyote

Western painted turtle

Green-winged teal

Tadpole

Daphnia

Dragonfly larva

Elodea

Algae

The Sun as a Source of Light

Advantage	Disadvantage
available for free	if indoors and there are no windows, cannot use the Sun to see
shines all day	does not shine at night

◀ A **T-chart** shows two sides of a topic.

Communicating Using Tables and Graphs

Creating Data Tables

Data tables are used to write your observations. Data is the information you collected. In this table, the data is weather facts, such as temperature and precipitation. Data tables are a good way to organize your information.

Weather Log						
Date						
Time						
Temperature—current						
Temperature—high						
Temperature—low						
Precipitation type						
Precipitation amount						
Cloud cover						
Wind speed						
Wind direction						
Air pressure						

Graphing Data

Sometimes you read graphs to find information. This is called interpreting data. When you conduct an investigation or do research, you collect data. Sometimes the patterns or relationships in the data are hard to see. Looking at a graph makes it easier to see the information.

Bar Graphs

A **bar graph** shows relationships between separate sets of data. It is a way to show data that uses horizontal or vertical bars. Look at the bar graph here. It shows the rainfall in different months of the year.

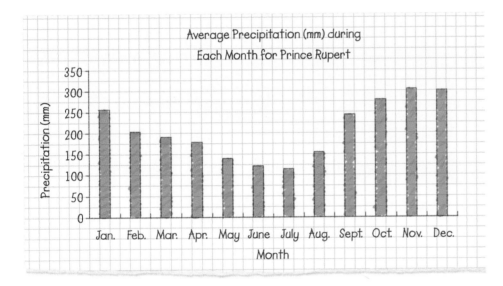

Line Graphs

A **line graph** is useful when you are looking at a relationship between two different things. It shows changes in measurement over time. The line graph for the data here helps you see that temperatures changed depending on the month.

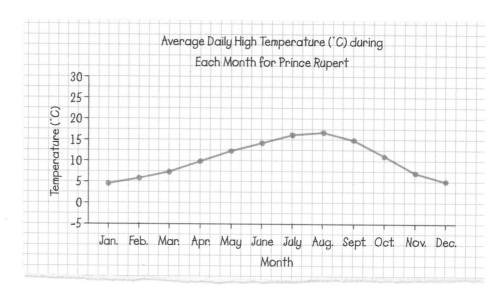

Circle Graphs

A **circle graph** (or pie graph) shows the whole of something divided into all its parts. A circle graph is round and compares data by showing it as parts of the circle. This circle graph shows favourite extreme weather events of students in a class.

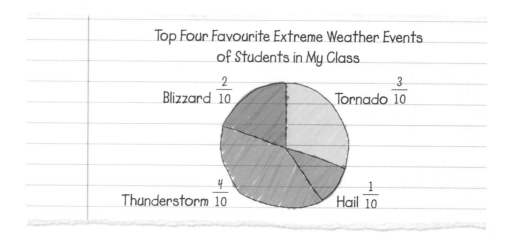

Glossary

A

absorb to soak up something, such as light or sound

adaptation the way in which an organism is suited to its habitat

air pressure the weight of the air pushing on you

anemometer an instrument used to measure wind speed; measures wind speed in kilometres per hour (km/h)

artificial made by humans; not natural; for example, light from a lamp is artificial

B

barometer an instrument used to measure changes in air pressure

C

carnivore an animal that eats other animals; for example, a frog is a carnivore

cirrus clouds thin, feather-like clouds that sit high in the sky and are made up of ice crystals

climate the general weather pattern or normal weather for a particular place; determined by measuring average temperature and precipitation over a long period of time

cloud a mass of tiny water droplets that have condensed from water vapour in the air

community two or more populations that live together in the same habitat

condensation the process of water vapour turning into liquid water

conservation plans to stop further damage to a habitat; putting litter in the garbage, eating unpackaged foods, and turning off the lights when you're not home are examples of conservation

consumer an organism that eats plants or animals or both as food; animals are consumers

cumulus clouds fluffy clouds with flat bottoms; often tall and piled high like stacked cotton puffs

E

echo the sound heard when a sound wave is reflected back from a hard surface

endangered plant and animal populations that are in danger of disappearing forever because of extreme changes in a habitat

energy the ability to do work; can be seen in the form of light and heard in the form of sound

erosion the movement of rock and soil from one place to another

evaporation the process of liquid water turning into water vapour

extinct an organism no longer living anywhere on Earth; dinosaurs are an example of an organism that has become extinct

F

food chain a diagram of who eats whom in a community

food web a diagram of how producers, consumers, and scavengers are connected in a habitat

frequency the number of vibrations per second

H

habitat the home of an organism; the ocean, a forest, and a tree are all habitats

herbivore an animal that only eats plants; for example, beavers are herbivores

I

Indigenous Knowledge (IK) understandings about the natural world unique to a particular group or culture who have lived for a very long time in that area; this knowledge is passed to the next generation through stories and songs

L

light beam a group of many light rays

loudness how loud or soft a sound is; depends on the size of the vibrations of a sound wave

N

natural present in or produced by nature; not artificial; for example, light produced by the Sun is natural

O

omnivore an animal that eats both plants and animals; for example, grizzly bears are omnivores

opaque blocking all light from passing through it; for example, a solid wood door is opaque

organism a living thing; plants and animals are organisms

P

pitch how high or low a sound is; depends on the number of sound vibrations per second

population all the members of one type of plant or animal in a habitat

precipitation water that falls from the sky to Earth in the form of rain, snow, or hail

predator an animal that hunts other animals for food; for example, sea otters are predators

prey an organism that is hunted by a predator; for example, sea urchins are prey to sea otters

prism a transparent piece of glass or plastic that can split light into a spectrum

producer an organism that can produce its own food; plants are producers

R

rain gauge an instrument used to measure rainfall; measures rainfall in millimetres (mm)

reflect to bounce off an object; light can reflect off a mirror

refract to bend and change direction of light; occurs when light enters a material at an angle and then slows down; water refracts light

S

scavenger an animal that eats animals that are dying or already dead; for example, crows are scavengers

sound anything that can be heard; for example, music from a stereo, popcorn popping in a microwave, and cars on the street all make sound

sound wave each vibration in an object that produces sound

spectrum a band of colours that occurs when light is refracted and split; colours in the spectrum are red, orange, yellow, green, blue, and violet

stratus clouds flat, layered clouds; usually seen on a grey day

T

temperature the measure of the energy produced by the Sun that heats the surface of Earth

thermometer an instrument used to measure temperature; measures temperature in degrees Celsius (°C)

threatened plant and animal populations that are in danger because of negative changes in a habitat; threatened plant and animal populations may become endangered if negative change is not stopped

translucent allowing some light to pass through, but not enough to see clearly through; frosted glass and wax paper are translucent

transmit allow to pass through; for example, a window will transmit light

transparent transmitting light and allowing you to clearly see through; water is transparent

V

vibration quick back-and-forth movement; an object must vibrate to make sound

vocal cords two bands of tissue in your throat that vibrate to produce sound

volume the loudness of a sound

W

water cycle the recycling of water on Earth through evaporation, condensation, and precipitation

weather the day-to-day changes of Earth's atmosphere

weather vane an instrument used to measure wind direction; also called a wind vane

wind moving air

wind direction the direction from which wind is coming; for example, a south wind comes from the south

wind speed the measure of how fast wind is moving

Index

Credits

Front Cover
Martin Rugner/AGE Foto Stock/firstlight.ca.

Table of Contents
iv-v Michael Orton/Stone/Getty Images; vi-vii Albert Normandin/Masterfile; viii-ix Altrendo Nature/Getty Images.

Preface
p. 1 Courtesy of Lee George, Sliammon Salmonid Enhancement Society.

Unit A
Unit A Opener pp. 2-3 Michael Orton/Stone/Getty Images; p. 4 Gunter Marx Photography/Corbis Canada; p. 14 left Tony Freeman/Photo Edit; right Courtesy of Boreal Laboratories; p. 17 top to bottom Damir Frkovic/Masterfile; Brian Stablyk/Getty Images; David Muench/Corbis Canada; Russell Monk/Masterfile; p. 19 top Gunter Marx Photography; bottom left Michael Melford/NGS Collection/Getty Images; bottom right Chris Noble/Photographer's Choice/Getty Images; p. 21 Courtesy of Boreal Laboratories; p. 22 left H. Riola/AGE Foto Stock/firstlight.ca; right Patrick Coughlin/Stone/Getty Images; p. 24 Courtesy of Boreal Laboratories; p. 30 David Young-Wolff/Photo Edit; p. 32 Ward Perrin/Vancouver Sun; p. 33 Gabe Palmer/Corbis Canada; p. 34 Courtesy of International Institute for Sustainable Development; p. 37 Al Harvey/The Slide Farm; p. 44 top Reuters/Corbis Canada; bottom Andy Clark/Reuters/Corbis Canada; p. 46 David R. Frazier/Photo Researchers, Inc.; p. 47 top Darryl Torckler/Taxi/Getty Images; bottom Courtesy of Pat Wong, Science Division, MSC PYR; p. 49 bottom left Corbis Canada; right Courtesy of Pat Wong, Science Division, MSC PYR; p. 54 Richard Lam/CP Photo; p. 55 Bill Lowry/Ivy Images; p. 57 left George Herben/Visuals Unlimited; right Tom Evans/AlaskaStock.com; p. 58 Chase Swift/Corbis Canada; p. 59 Charles George/Visuals Unlimited; p. 60 top Gunter Marx Photography; bottom left Thomas Kitchin & Victoria Hurst/firstlight.ca; bottom right Jack Ballard/Visuals Unlimited; p. 61 left Betts Anderson Loman/Photo Edit; right Bill Lowry/Ivy Images; p. 62 top left Timothy Shonnard/Stone/Getty Images; top centre Gary Gerovac/Masterfile; top right Jeff Schultz/AlaskaStock.com; bottom left Emma Bazinet, photo by Jean-Claude Bazinet; right Edward S. Curtis/Corbis Canada; p. 64 top left R. Schabl/Masterfile; bottom right B&C Alexander Photography, www.arcticphoto.co.uk; p. 65 left Gordon Peterson/firstlight.ca; centre Brian A. Vikander/Corbis Canada; right Courtesy of Don Mann, Granby Post & Beam Homes; p. 66 left Richard Lam/CP Photo; top right Michael Orton/Stone/Getty Images; bottom right Courtesy of KidzCanDo.com; p. 67 top Manfred Thonig/firstlight.ca; bottom left Olivier Mackay/firstlight.ca; bottom right Reuters/Corbis Canada; p. 68 top Greg Stott/Masterfile; bottom Inga Spence/Visuals Unlimited; p. 70 David Collier/Getty Images.

Unit B
Unit B Opener pp. 78-79 Albert Normandin/Masterfile; p. 80 Roger Ressmeyer/Corbis Canada; p. 81 top Kevin Cozad/O'Brien Productions/Corbis Canada; p. 82 left Courtesy of NASA; right G. Schuster/zefa/Corbis Canada; p. 83 Eckard Slawik/Science Photo Library; p. 84 top left Chris Madeley/Photo Researchers, Inc.; top right Michael Orton/Stone/Getty Images; bottom left Alfio Scigliano/Sygma/Corbis Canada; bottom right Jerry Lodriguss/Photo Researchers, Inc.; p. 85 left Jean-Marie Bassot/Photo Researchers, Inc.; right Y. Kito/Image Quest 3-D; p. 86 left Darwin Dale/Photo Researchers, Inc; right Harbor Branch Oceanographic Institute; p. 87 top left Peter Herring/Image Quest 3-D; right Chris Parks/Image Quest 3-D; bottom left E. Widder/Visuals Unlimited; p. 88 David Young-Wolff/Photo Edit; p. 89 top left Thomas Del Brase/Stone/Getty Images; top centre Tony Freeman/Photo Edit; top right Plainpicture/firstlight.ca; bottom left (top) Elizabeth Knox/Masterfile; bottom left (bottom) Kevin Morris/Corbis Canada; bottom centre Richard Treptow/Photo Researchers, Inc./firstlight.ca; bottom right Dave Robertson/

SENATOR REID ELEMENTARY
9341 - 126th STREET
SURREY, B.C.
V3V 5C4